❖ IS THE LAST SUPPER FINISHED?

❖ Is the Last Supper Finished?

SECULAR LIGHT ON A SACRED MEAL

by Arthur A. Vogel

with a Preface by Bernard Cooke, S.J.

SHEED AND WARD: NEW YORK

To K. A. V.

ACKNOWLEDGMENTS   Portions of the Introduction and of Chapters I and II were delivered as the McMath Lectures in Detroit, Michigan, 1967. Unless otherwise noted, all quotations from the Bible are from the Revised Standard Version, copyrighted 1946 and 1952 by the Division of Christian Education, National Council of the Churches of Christ in the U.S.A.

❖ Preface

It was almost inevitable that this book would be strongly ecumenical in tone because of Fr. Vogel's deep involvement in ecumenical developments throughout the world. But today it is no great news when a book on theology is ecumenically directed; we now expect that. Nor is it particularly surprising that with his ecumenical interests the author has decided to explain the action of Christian Eucharist.

The further we advance in serious ecumenical dialogue the more it becomes clear that the action of the Eucharist and the ministry which is exercised in it stand at the very focus of the questions that separate the various Christian Churches one from another. The action of the Eucharist is meant to be a key sign of Christian unity and until it becomes that rather than a source of division one cannot expect any real healing of the breach which now exists among Christians. It is in this context obviously of the importance of the Eucharist that increasing interest has been expressed in the possibilities of inter-communion. This inter-communion will not of itself constitute Christian reunion in the full sense, but it may very well be a major step in that direction.

Yet there is a grave danger that theological discussion of ecumenism, of the Eucharist, of inter-communion, may become very provincial, even narcissistic. What may happen is that just as we achieve reunification among Christians, just as we gather to celebrate Eucharist together, we may find that in our contemporary world this is an irrelevant and futile gesture. Beyond the questions of reunion and the role of Christian worship in this reunion, stands the imposing question of contemporary faith or unbelief. For anyone who writes seriously and meaningfully on the Eucharist at the present time there arises the inescapably fundamental question: What does the Eucharist—or for that matter the Church as a whole—say to our world? What does it have to offer to our emerging cultures? What contribution can it make to our contemporary evolution of thought?

Here precisely lies the interest and the value of Fr. Arthur Vogel's book. His broad acquaintance with phenomenology and contemporary existentialist thought gives him a vantage point from which he can view the Christian realities of Church and Sacrament in typically contemporary fashion. Familiar as he is with the outlooks and questions of contemporary thought and literature, he brings these to bear on an appraisal of Christian life and on Christian liturgy as an integral part of that life.

One notices in theologians like Fr. Vogel, who draw heavily from contemporary psychological and phenomenological thought, a marked capacity to integrate the activity of sacramental liturgy and the other activities of human life. Herein lies one of the most promising and exciting hopes for the development of sacramental theology today. We have always known that there is some relationship between human life in its totality and the Christian sacramental system, but we have done little to clarify our understanding of that relationship. Yet it is intrinsic to Christian sacrament, above all to the Eucharist, to be inextricably intertwined with the most basic of human experiences—death, birth, love, sorrow, sinfulness —and to transform these experiences by the Christ-mystery at the very same time that it is using these experiences to understand what the Christ-mystery is all about.

This may seem to be downgrading the importance of liturgy and laying stress almost exclusively on "ordinary daily actions." But so to interpret this theological development is to miss the point. Actually, an unbreakable continuity exists between specifically liturgical acts of sacrament and the rest of human life, so that sacraments would be utterly unintelligible, as a matter of fact impossible, were there not the other human experiences on which they build. And on the other hand, a Christian meaning of human life could never be known by man if the experience of sacrament were totally missing.

Fr. Vogel's book is a non-technical but scholarly addition to the literature that is gradually clarifying for us this understanding of Christian life and Christian worship as one integrated process of Christian experience. Hopefully, it will make the experience of being a Christian much more realistic and relevant for a large number of readers.

BERNARD COOKE, s.j.

❖ Contents

Contents

❖ IS THE LAST SUPPER FINISHED?

✤ Introduction

By almost universal assent the most important questions facing Christians today are these: How should the Church be related to secular reality? How can the Church be related to the secular world?

The answer to both questions must be, "By being itself."

But what self is the Church? What is the key to its nature? What is the basic structure of Christianity?

I think the answer to those questions is found in the Holy Eucharist, also known as the Holy Communion, the Lord's Supper, the Mass.

To many people that answer may seem disappointing and provincial; it may seem too small for the size of the problems confronting us. The answer will appear to be "the same old thing" at best and totally inadequate at worst. For some the Last Supper is finished.

Actually, the biggest problem in Christianity today may be that the Holy Eucharist can be thought of as either a small or provincial answer to the questions we have just posed. When its nature is understood, the Holy Eucharist exists to challenge every liturgical church, every nonliturgical church, and even people who are not Christian at all. It *is* Christianity in the world. The topic this book discusses is inclusive enough to take on the world at the world's fullest and contemporary enough to hurl a total challenge to our age. Our theme is not an exercise in yesterday's piety.

No greater condemnation can be made of Christendom than this: the Holy Eucharist, intended key to Christianity's radical application in the world, has become a stumbling block to those within and without the Church. The key to Christian living seems only to fit a two-thousand-year-old door that no forward-looking person wants to enter if he is feeling well. The Eucharist is a stumbling block to many people within the Church because, although they try to use it, they do not understand it well enough to use it correctly. Non-Christians, and some who think of themselves as Christians, misunderstand it and do not even want to use it. In either case, the key is lost.

I contend that the Eucharist, properly understood, is the focus of Christian living, especially appropriate for present-day men. In an age of cybernation when our central nervous system is being extended by electric circuits and when—we are told—the recognition of patterns, instead of the laborious gathering of data, promises to assume a dominating role in our lives, the Holy Eucharist offers us a unique pattern for Christian living.

Our understanding of the Lord's Supper also deeply affects the ecumenical movement in which churches are now engaged. Many people believe that the goal of Christian unity is the common sharing of the sacrament of the Holy Eucharist; however, if that is the case, and if the

Holy Communion continues to mean to most people what it means today, union among Christian churches will be a flop even if it is achieved. As things stand, we are in danger of making nothing more than a church service the goal of reunion when we say that the Eucharist is its goal. If we go to Holy Communion together after reunion and the eucharistic action is no more pervasive in the world then than it is now, there will be no point to reunion. The goal of ecumenism is not to make the same thing we now have available in more places; it is to make us different everywhere. That is why there can be no reunion without renewal. We and our churches are not worth uniting unless they are more than they are now. The goal of reunion is service and witness in the world, not more convenient consumption of sacramental food in our church buildings.

The Lord's table is not the Christian equivalent of Procrustes' bed, requiring us to be less than ourselves in order to fit it. The Eucharist is not a quaint activity requiring us to state our problems in its terms if it is to help us; for if we will look deeply enough into the Eucharist's structure, we will find our terms already there. The Holy Eucharist is not an otherworldly activity handed down to us from on high for which we have to go out and find significance. It works upon our being from within that being, not from without. If those claims can be substantiated, we will have shown why the Eucharist is so radical, why it is so new, why it is so contemporary, why it is so necessary for every man.

The Eucharist, I suggest, is the key to our lives because we are the key to it. We are not its key in the sense of being able completely to account for it by ourselves, for it involves the grace-filled activity of God. Still we can be its key in the sense of being the ones commissioned to use it and the ones whom it fits; we explain it in the sense that it is uniquely *for* us. God's coming to us in Christ and in the Holy Eucharist fits us so well that all of our nature is involved. That is why Christ's words "Do this in remembrance of me" (I Corinthians 11:24 f.; Luke 22:19) can supply a complete program for our lives.

Converging insights about the nature of man as a person are a striking feature of our day. Many sociologists, anthropologists, psychologists, and philosophers find themselves saying much the same thing about man; students are beginning to discover similar truths taught in different departments of their universities. The consensus of which I speak has now been developing long enough for relatively stable features to appear. It is safe to say, accordingly, that by almost universal agreement today man can be understood as a person in the world only through his participation in community, language, and body. He can be himself only through those dimensions of being.

In a most striking way, those basic aspects of man also lie at the heart of the Eucharist; they are the Eucharist's characteristic tissue, or structure, found both in its worldly root and divine flowering. The eucharistic meal is the intimate activity and expression of the Christian community of faith; as such it essentially involves man's communal, social nature. The eucharistic food is called the Body of Christ; in that light, it makes immediate reference to man's body. Moreover, the eucharistic Body is said to be the presence of the incarnate Word; thus man's words and the meaning he participates in through them are also involved in it.

The Eucharist perfects human activity because it is based upon that activity; it springs from nothing less than man's whole communal, linguistic, and bodily structure. Investigation will show those to be ubiquitous aspects of human existence, and the degree of our participation in the Eucharist is meant to be as ubiquitous as they. Everything we do involving community, language, and our bodies should be our eucharistic participation. Since those dimensions of our being are big, even total, our involvement in the Eucharist is meant to be big, even total.

It is impossible to go to a church service once a week and then try to act the rest of the week as if one were still there. That is what many people try to do, however, in their attempts to live eucharistic lives. Until we can see that the Eucharist is more than a church service, we can hardly expect better consequences than discontinuous church services can produce, namely, a divided Christendom and a world unconvinced of Christ's lordship.

Given to us as it was, the Eucharist uses what we are in order to make us what we are not. When seen in its true perspective, for example, the Eucharist does not take us as isolated individuals and try to make us socially minded and concerned with one another. It is rather a taking of us as we cannot help but be—social creatures, already interdependent on one another and on the world—in order to make *those* relationships godly in a new sense. An obvious problem of our day, however, is to realize the intimate dependence we have on each other and on the world.

What we call "society" seems to be the very thing producing impersonal relations and antisocial behavior; we are often hard put to find any element in a given person's life on which the doctrine of the Eucharist can be anchored.

To the extent that we do not realize the interpersonal constitution of our being, the eucharistic perfection God wills for us will seem foreign to us. In the pages that follow we shall examine the interpersonal aspects of the selves we cannot help but be, as those aspects have been revealed by some of the latest developments in the human sciences. Until the truth of these insights becomes an acknowledged dimension of our twenty-four-hour-a-day lives, we will not be able to participate fully in the eucharistic activity Christ commissioned us to perform.

The body is another key to a radical, contemporary understanding of the Eucharist. Christians have long said that salvation depends upon a person's relation to the mystical Body of Christ (the Church) and a person's cooperation with the action producing the sacramental Body (the Holy Eucharist). What meaningful approach can we take to these subjects other than the experience we have of our own bodies? The bodily analogies lying at the heart of the Christian doctrine of the Church and the Holy Eucharist are based upon man's relation to his body. If we approach these fundamental Christian images through our own bodily lives, we will be approaching them through the reality from which they were originally drawn; in addition, we will be dealing with them through our own most immediate experience. Then we won't have to search for relevance in our religion; we will begin with relevance.

Considerations of Christ's mystical body and of his eucharistic body are meaningful to us through the "privileged experience" we have of our own bodies. There is a primacy of the *now*, of our immediate experience, for all meaning. All appeals to us are not on the same footing; if an appeal is made to us, it must be through the way we experience ourselves in the world. Our experience does not coincide with everything that is real, but that experience is the only vehicle we have for relating to reality; it is our only means of personal growth.

We experience nothing else with the same immediacy with which we experience our bodies; that experience is the ever-present landscape of everything else we do. Nothing can replace it; all things somehow involve it. It furnishes the primary meaning of life in the world, to which all other meaning is related. If we can approach our relation to the Eucharist through the experience of our bodies, realizing through that experience the basic meaning of life in Christ's mystical body and the role of the sacramental body, we will have a "privileged" insight into the nature of Christian living.

Must we not say that God chose to have the Church and Eucharist variously known as Christ's *body* just so we men can have a privileged relationship to them? What else could follow from God's decision to "become man," to reveal his Word in *flesh?*

Expression through language is the most telling and powerful ingredient in human culture. We seem to be inserted into reality through language much as we are inserted into reality through the body. We learn to use language from within; it is not something outside of us in the sense of being foreign to us, even though our linguistic ability is not fully actualized in our earliest years. We are born into a field of meaning, verbal and preverbal, that precedes us in our families and our cultures, but as we learn to speak we do not feel that we are becoming different from ourselves. We feel we are becoming more ourselves. Our being at home in language is our being at home with other people, through whose agency language is actualized in us.

Language, like our body, enables us to handle things. Moreover, the "body" of our language determines what we can handle. Our worlds are correlative to our language; the features of our worlds depend largely upon the aspects and dimensions of reality the language we use emphasizes. The worlds of poetry, physics, and history differ from each other because the language each one uses differs from the others.

Communities and languages grow together. Languages arise from our interrelations with one another and with nature; on the other hand, language enables us to have interrelations with one another and with nature. Language is a means of organization and direction; without man's linguistic ability to distinguish tasks and organize efforts, our contemporary world would be impossible. Some people think the contemporary world makes Christianity impossible. I think it is more likely that only the Christian Word can make possible a radically new contemporary world!

All the points we have been discussing need further elaboration; that elaboration will be attempted in the remainder of this book. At least my primary contention should now be clear: the features of our lives we have just noted—communal, corporeal, and linguistic—are the foundations in our being on which the Eucharist is anchored and from which it obtains its human intrigue. Those features enable the Eucharist to be meaningful to contemporary man and are the means by which all men, whether they be called Christians or not, participate in the activity consecrated by Christ in his consecration to the Father (cf. John 17:18 f.).

If the nature of the Eucharist is as I have described it, narrow provincialism of any kind is impossible in Christian living. We cannot participate in Christ's self-giving death through the eucharistic liturgy and then try to protect ourselves by his Food. In the mystical and sacramental bodies of Christ, God is among us still doing his work, i.e., creating the world. In offering himself to us in the Eucharist, God asks not for our protection but for our total commitment to him, to others, and to the world. The Eucharist commits us to God wherever we are ourselves, which is to say, wherever we are related to others through language and our bodies. The cosmic work of the Eucharist is a work we immediately share with all men simply by living in the same world with them; it is in that work that we are called to view all men and our relations with them.

In the dynamic view of reality modern man is convinced he must take, in which he understands that God's work is not finished and that God is still creating his world through human activity, protection of God by man's "piety" loses any propriety it might once have been thought to possess. Creation itself is an act of commitment and availability on God's part; so is the re-creation of the world through Christ's life and death on the cross. Because God's creation and redemption are continuing acts, God's commitment and availability to the world continue with the same totality Christ's death expressed. In the Eucharist we are called to "proclaim the Lord's death until he comes" (I Corinthians 11:26). Through the Eucharist we are extensions of Christ's vulnerability, sustained by the food of his victory; we are not guards placed at the door of his anteroom to protect him from profanation or contact with the world.

Christ was sent into the world for the world; the eucharistic banquet he inaugurated is in the world for the world, too. The Lord's Supper is so much in and for the world that it may truly be called a secular supper; in fact, it is so secular that it cannot be limited to the activities we usually associate with suppers! That is why it can be a Christian's life, something to be done everywhere, all the time, with everything and everyone.

I ✳ Reality

Acceptance of the real world is the first condition for being a Christian.

A person is himself only in a world, and he can be his full self only in the real world. Reality qualifies the nature of everything in our lives, even our fantasies; what we escape to is determined by the reality we want to escape from, and once we do escape we are, in reality, escapists.

The Christian life is not an escape mechanism. Christianity is either the means of being our real selves in the real world or it is nothing. There are those to whom it is nothing or, at best, as Freud thought, a real illusion. Accordingly, before proceeding to a detailed discussion of the Christian life as it is epitomized in the Eucharist, we should dispel all false notions about the general relation of Christianity to reality. Above all, we must be clear about the primacy of reality in our lives and about Christianity's relation to that primacy.

Involvement with reality carries its own confirmation with it. That is the consuming satisfaction materialists find in their lives and which, unfortunately, many people who are called religious miss in theirs. A seemingly nonreligious person committing himself in the world may have a more complete personal life, because he is more fully himself, than someone who is known as a Christian but who is motivated primarily by fear and self-protection. The latter is worried about himself; the former is being himself.

I have a friend who for a long time refused to fly when he traveled. He said that he would fly if necessary, but clever planning always enabled him to keep the necessity from arising. He could even find a reason for avoiding a trip altogether if flying was the only way he could make it. Secretly his fear of flying was making him more and more disappointed with himself, and, as is always the case with psychological disguises, the casual attitude he tried to adopt with his friends only increased his inner tension. His struggle with himself continued for years, but he finally understood that his refusal to fly was an attempt to deny the true nature of his being, for exposure to risk is a condition of human life.

My friend decided that since he was in the world, he would try to accept that fact more completely. Intellectually, he knew the "statistical safety" of flying, that fewer people are killed per mile traveled by air than per mile traveled in automobiles. He repeated all the arguments to himself; but being abstract generalizations, they left him where they found him—on the ground. Goaded on by the realization that he was actually being less than himself instead of protecting himself by his conduct, he finally resolved to take his next trip by air. Once his decision was made, he reported, his life was easier than he had anticipated. He slept better the night before his first flight than he did on numerous other nights when, secretly perturbed by his cowardice, he knew that he could lie safely in bed all the next day if he wished. During the flight itself, he said, he was not without fear, although his experience could not be described as one of fear. He had a feeling of belonging; he knew in his whole being that because he was more completely in the world he was freer than he had ever been before. Participating more fully in the world, he was more fully himself; by exposing himself to a situation which would have terrified him if he thought about it alone at home, he was more than the self he was trying to protect at home.

Now, when my friend is forced back into his seat by the sudden thrust of a plane's engines, instead of worrying about all the things which could go wrong, he thinks how wonderful it is that man can develop engines so powerful. The unseen force momentarily rushing through his body, pressing his head against the back of his seat, has become his physical participation in an ongoing victory instead of a signal for withdrawal and self-concern.

Our being is thick, and we belong in the thick of things. There is a feeling of invulnerability that comes from being "in things." Considered from that point of view, exposure to danger may actually give us a settled feeling. If we acknowledge what we are, there is even a type of confirmation of our being in death. One way friends try to console a woman whose husband has died is to say, "Remember, death is as natural for us as life." In one sense that is certainly true, and, contrary to what a cynic may think, the remark is not one of desperation, made because others do not know what else to say; it is an insight of normalcy which even an abnormal person cannot miss under the circumstances. There is consolation simply in accepting the real. The real "belongs," and we know in our bones that we belong if we are real. Something in the core of our being refuses to accept the finality of pretending.

Imprisonment, by limiting a man's total involvement in the world, is an inverse way of emphasizing his need for such involvement. Longing for a fuller participation in the world than he can attain is a prisoner's punishment. After his imprisonment by the Nazis in the early 1940's, Dietrich Bonhoeffer, of whom we've heard so much in recent years, wrote to a friend that more than anything else he longed to tire of the sun rather than of books and of thought. He longed for bodily exposure to the sun and the physical experience of its warmth; he was not afraid to say that he needed his "animal existence awakened." Fully participating in the world we are at our strongest; that is the condition in which we are called to be religious: under the sun in broad daylight, in our strength, not just in our passivities and dark confinements.

Approximately a year after he was confined in the Tegel Prison in Berlin, Bonhoeffer wrote that although the meaning of things was often obscure, he found relief in knowing that, even though he did not see their purpose, some things were unavoidable and simply had to be endured. Enduring reality thus became the confirmation of his being, a mark of his authenticity.

A generation has now grown up which has no firsthand knowledge of Nazi concentration camps, but many of the individuals of that generation nevertheless feel imprisoned. Confined by the routine way of life of an apathetic society, these young people feel a need to realize the wholeness of their being much as Bonhoeffer did. One method of such realization is the "happening," a term invented by a professor of the history of art, Allen Kaprow of New York. Mr. Kaprow's happenings are carefully planned and even proceed according to a script or "program." Some of them last for several days and require a number of different spatial locations.

One recent happening planned by Mr. Kaprow for a college campus involved such activities as students slowly marching in a circle carrying blank placards; sit-ins on paths and in public places such as classrooms and cafeterias; women hanging their clothes on lines in the school cafeteria and men burying the women's clothes later in the day while the women cheered; dancing to a loud rock-and-roll band in the evening while strobe lights flashed on and off. That was the first day's agenda. The second day had sprawling lie-ins in the school halls; a foghorn sounding every sixty seconds; automobiles blinking their lights, beeping their horns, and playing rock music on their radios; students shouting and banging on objects; and a concluding silent sit-in by couples facing each other while flares burned in the night. The title of the happening just described was "Interruption"; its purpose was to interrupt the automatic and mechanical way of life of a university in which the students are no more than numbers. Numbers don't bury brassieres. Regardless of the happening's title, *participation* was its purpose; it was something to *do* rather than to watch.

While Mr. Kaprow programs his happenings, other

people do not. On the whole, happenings are just the opposite of well-structured, logical presentations; instead, they are clusters of events emphasizing feeling and bodily experience at the expense of rational order. Besides on school campuses they may take place in theaters, at house parties, and occasionally in the streets. In the theater they consist of a series of short acts succeeding one another in arbitrary fashion. The entire production can be described as occurring within the whole group present rather than as being a show performed before an audience; again, participation and a sense of bodily involvement are the key. Nontheatrical happenings on a less pretentious scale than Mr. Kaprow's have involved pouring water over people, squirting one another with hoses, rolling in paint on large canvasses, keeping wet clothes on, bathing in public, eating and drinking in exaggerated ways, smoking, burying people's bodies in sand or paper, reclining together, dancing, jumping, running, and having rooms illuminated by a revolving color wheel of light.

Happenings have been analyzed as nothing more than attempts to play with modes of perception, but through all their apparent madness a protest is being made by those who take part in them against the impersonal and often abstract world of our scientific and cybernetic age.

The confirmation of one's being through physical experience can also be illustrated by a practice common among isolated juvenile delinquents, tattooing themselves. During lonely periods of confinement they frequently tattoo designs and initials on their skin by poking it with a sharp pencil or some other such instrument and filling the wounds with ink or dirt. When asked why they engage in such painful activity, they often reply that it helps them feel real and personally present. Their quest for reality may not be adequate to their needs, but their action does emphasize the necessary relationship that exists between endurance and reality. Even self-inflicted pain can perversely hint at one's authentic being.

Bonhoeffer's imprisonment helped him discover how thoroughly we men need the reality of the world, even if the world's reality presents us with problems. We can learn to believe, Bonhoeffer thought, only by taking life in stride, that is, by accepting as our starting point the experiences of life as they come, be they successes or failures, duties or problems, achievements or helplessness. He advocated accepting the real world as a means of accepting true Christianity.

Reality and freedom go together. My friend who had feared flying said that he felt freer in the world after he had flown because he was more completely in the world. Our freedom is located in a reality that extends beyond us; to the extent that we try to deny the nature of that reality by our lives, to that extent it becomes impossible for us to be free.

Taking off in an airplane involves a commitment of oneself to more than oneself; when a plane starts down the runway, a person, including his most isolating self-concern, is obviously carried by something beyond him. Such a reference beyond himself is the way a person's being as a whole is related to the world every moment of his life. That is why the experience of flying can confirm a person's whole relation to the world—and to God. One such event can transform a life by highlighting for the first time a relationship that has been present but unnoticed.

Christians need the sense of belonging *here* that an atheist has—or should have. We need to be settled where we are, like flour shaken down in a bowl; we need to accept the fact that there is no alternative to reality, as reality already exists. That, above all else, is what the atheist knows: things are not different from what they are, and we are not different from ourselves.

It is because some Christians have learned for the first time the total acceptance of reality that we hear so much these days about "Christian atheism." The enthusiasm people have for that term indicates their enthusiasm for accepting the reality of the world with no reservations. So understood, "Christian atheism" is not the contradiction it at first appears to be. Enthusiasts do not mind bearing the label of a school or person from whom they have learned something important; many Christians are presently learning something important about the acceptance of the world from those who do not accept God.

Hoping that something which is not here is here is the shortest road to agony. "If I were not so old, I would have a chance to make a brilliant discovery before I was thirty, when brilliant discoveries are supposed to be made," muses the associate professor. He is miserable at forty-five because he wants still to be in his twenties at forty-five. "I could snap that pretty face up right now if I weren't married," are the thoughts of a man who longs to be single at the very moment he is married.

It is not my claim that atheists are models of marital fidelity or of contentment in a career or profession; but atheism, by the simple method of denying any alternative to it, does secure total acceptance of the world. Lack of an *alternative* to reality is atheism's great insight.

Christians who have quit praying and claim that they find themselves better for it are perhaps discovering that same insight for the first time. To the extent that the insight is a true one, it confirms their being and they consequently feel enthusiastic about it. There is no point in denying that much of what passes for prayer is actually reverie and wish projection; Christians must learn that such so-called "prayer" contradicts both their nature and God's.

Perhaps the way I have discussed atheism's virtue seems to go too far. Actually not. I have merely been stressing the fact that there are no genuine alternatives to reality for anyone, including Christians. We frequently face alternatives in life; but they are *through* reality, not *to* it. The primacy of reality is the only basis for Christian hope. God gave himself to us in Christ just so that we would not have to purchase hope in him at the price of denying the reality of the world.

There are real problems in the world, and they are as real for Christians as they are for atheists. To be human means to share common problems; to be Christian, on the other hand, means to embody a special answer to those problems. "Why does God permit evil in the world?" is not a question Christians should be expected to answer. No human being knows an alternative to the world, but the question implies that there should be such an alternative at the very moment we are in the world. The basic dissatisfaction involved is the same as that of the man who wants to be twenty when he is forty-five. In both instances, the questioner had better get with reality, for there is no alternative to it.

The question about evil implies that if God is good and omnipotent, he should have made the world differently than he did. A favorite pastime of nonbelievers is finding theological students to whom they can direct God's question: "Why is reality the way it is?" But a theological student takes his work in divinity too seriously if he thinks he can answer God's question. Students take their degrees in the midst of a world racked by pain and problems; they do not get their degrees because they made such a world. The Christian answer to the condition of the world is not to deny the world's nature but to show that more can be done through the world than would be possible if there were no God.

Questions about evil in the world are at best theoretical and at worst symptomatic of a desire to escape reality. Since, in the end, reality cannot be escaped by either the Christian or the non-Christian, it should be equally accepted by both in the beginning. The result of such acceptance is that the only legitimate answer to the existential problem of evil is an existential attitude in its presence. To struggle against disaster, a total affirmation of our being, is the only appropriate response we can give to the problem.

In Camus' novel *The Plague*, a deadly epidemic unexpectedly hits the Algerian coastal town of Oran. Reactions to the disaster differ among the townspeople, but the story settles on a Dr. Rieux and his friends and acquaintances, who, for various reasons and at different times, spend themselves struggling against the catastrophe.

Dr. Rieux is the most constant and unflinching worker of all. From time to time he is asked why he exposes himself so completely in his efforts, why he is so devoted to his work. It is not, he replies, that he believes in God. He had searched for him, but had never found him. If he had found an all-powerful God, the doctor said, he would leave the curing of the sick to God. Even Christians do not believe in such a God, he continued, because none of them ever completely throws himself on Providence. The best resolution of the human condition Dr. Rieux could arrive at was "fighting against creation as he found it." God, if he is in heaven, is silent; all Dr. Rieux knew is that sick people exist and that they need curing. What is first needed in a world confronted with disease and "shaped by death" is struggle against them; later we can think things over and get our theories straight.

Rambert, a journalist from Paris, is trapped in Oran by the plague; his only desire is to escape the town in which he does not belong and return to the woman he loves. There is no possibility of his leaving Oran by legal means, so he tries to pave the way for an escape by bribing some young border guards. Dr. Rieux knows of Rambert's plans, but he does not make the least effort to try to dissuade him. The doctor even tells Rambert that he is absolutely right in his desires. After having said that, Dr. Rieux adds that the only reason for fighting a plague, and the only means of such a fight, is common decency. People might smile, but it is as simple as that.

Men who volunteered for work in "sanitary squads," groups that moved the stricken, disposed of corpses, and otherwise ministered to the hygienic needs of the city, do not come in for extreme praise by the chronicler of the disaster. Their heroism is minimized by the fact that they did the only thing to do in the circumstances. It would have been "unthinkable" that these people would not have done their job. The logic of the situation was too basic and simple for praise; it would make as much sense to praise a schoolteacher for teaching that two plus two equals four. The plague was a fact, and the necessity of fighting against it was equally a fact. All one had to know was that two plus two equals four.

Camus has described the problems of evil and death in the world with a violence few have exceeded. His vivid descriptions of the death agonies of victims of the plague, including children, preclude any equally convincing theoretical explanations of why such things should be—as Paneloux, the priest in the story, finally has to admit. That, however, is precisely the point I have been trying to make: Christians and non-Christians start in the same place. They must equally accept the reality of death, pain, and suffering. Neither has an advantage over the other in that respect.

Christianity is not an abstract theory about the world that tries to disguise the world or explain its difficulties away. Dr. Rieux's personal answer to the plague by throwing himself against it, existence answering existence, is actually the texture of the Christian answer to evil. That explains why some who do not call themselves Christians are closer to Christianity than others who covet the name. Texture, not labels, determines who are men of Christian cloth.

To be a knowing Christian, Dr. Rieux would have had only to realize that Providence is not a bed men can throw themselves upon (Christianity's chief symbol is a cross, not a mattress), nor is creation something finished which we can fight against. For Christians, the creation of God's world is still going on through men, and Providence is the name of the process!

The essence of Christianity is *to live in God's world, the real world, which is still in the making.* We have been discussing the reality of the world because we must not think that the world is God's at the expense of reality. The mark of our belief in God is the acceptance of reality, not its denial.

God transcends the universe, but he does his work in the universe from the inside out. Christian faith works from within the world, and by so doing, to use a term made current by Teilhard de Chardin, it *sur-animates* the nature of the world. Teilhard speaks of God working through "the deep being of things," which means that

the manifestation of the divine no more modifies the apparent order of things than the eucharistic consecration modifies the sacred Species to our eyes . . . the relations between creatures remains exactly the same. They are merely accentuated in meaning. Like those translucent materials which a light within them can illuminate as a whole . . . the great mystery of Christianity is not exactly the appearance, but the transparence, of God in the universe. Yes, Lord, not only the ray that strikes the surface, but the ray that penetrates, not only Your Epiphany, Jesus, but *Your diaphany*.[1]

It cannot be denied that all the problems confronting us

[1] Pierre Teilhard de Chardin, *The Divine Milieu: An Essay on the Interior Life* (New York: Harper and Row, 1960), p. 110.

today have been produced within the course of the universe's development; the universe's past and our participation in its present are the common heritage of all men. Now, however, because of Christ's coming into the world, Christians claim that men can discover the final solution to their problems immanently within the same ongoing process. The Christian solution to our problems comes to us in the same type of existence which produced the problems in the first place.

That insight is the basis of Teilhard's great appeal for contemporary man. Teilhard sees the type of reality Christianity must have if it is to be true: it must be at least as real as the material forces working in the evolution of the universe. Taken in that general sense, Teilhard's intentions seem to be both correct and Christian. Teilhard does not see God's answer to man's problems in terms which deny our location in, or rupture our continuity with, the material universe; he gives the process of Christian redemption an essential relation to the processes of the natural world. Because he, like St. Paul, sees Jesus as the Cosmic Christ, Christian motivation can be described in cosmic terms, terms which everyone admits fit the problems of the cosmos. People are thus motivated by what is familiar to them and by what they know they are caught up in, the life of the all-inclusive universe. In those terms we do not feel dislocated or unreal in being religious; Christianity's homogeneity with us is acknowledged because it deals with us as the material realities we know we are.

Because of God's incarnation in Jesus Christ, the Christian solution of our problems must be felt at the same

level of reality at which we discover the problems: the
level of our bodily participation in the universe, of our
total self-expression, and of all of our human relations.
Jesus Christ took the reality of the world into himself to
give his reality to the world. That is why, after the Incarnation, no excuse can be tolerated for trying to live with
God at a level less complete than the fullness of the
world; that is why the Eucharist can be the paradigm of
Christian living. The world is something we begin in, not
build up to. Being secure enough to begin our lives where
we actually are is the first dimension of "living in God's
world."

Because God is incarnate, our love for him can be
known only in our action in the world. That is reasonable
enough, for Christians specifically know God's love for
them only in Christ's action in the world. We cannot take
too literally the words of I John 4:9, "*In this* the love of
God was made manifest among us, that God sent his only
Son into the world, so that we might live through him."
To live in the world is, as we have seen, to take a chance.
We either love God in the taking of worldly chances or
our love does not have the reality of the world—which
makes it no love at all.

To live in God's world means to live with God in the
richness of this world but rooted in a source deeper than
the world's own being. In Jesus Christ, God assures our
worldliness from within the world. From the time of Jesus
Christ onward, the conditions of our being have God's
guarantee; God in Christ has let himself become the
means of our accepting ourselves. Jesus saves us from the
internal tension of being worldly for the sake of the ten-

sions of the world! In Christ we are able to forget ourselves so that we can be more fully in the world—where
we are ourselves.

To live in God's world is to live in the real world; it is to
live with God in the reality of the world. "Living in God's
world" is the most intimate way we can live with God, for
every person, just by being himself, makes a world. Bill,
who loves Mary, feels his intimacy with her wherever he is
because, centering his world in her, he lives in her world.
Our worlds are our styles of life; Jesus Christ, God's style
of life for man, comes to us so that we can help in the
creation of God's world through our lives in him.

The Eucharist is the all-inclusive paradigm of Christ's
life. It is a total way of being in the world. To live eu-
charistically is to live in the Spirit, participating in a pattern of activity independent of us but one which is meant
to be realized only through us. We are not the center of
that pattern; instead, it centers us. It is a pattern bigger
than we are which includes all that we are. Participating
in it is to be with God in a way as big as reality itself;
participating in it we are also ever ready for a reality that
is bigger than the one we know today, for God in Christ
constantly transcends whatever we already are.

II ✤ "Face Me"

The centrality of Christ's words "This is my body" for the theme this book develops is obvious. That being the case, an examination of the role of the body in human life near the beginning of our study can hardly be unexpected. We are going to consider *community*, *word*, and *body* before we finish, and, although our final understanding would not be altered if we turned first to a consideration of community or word, there is an obvious propriety in beginning with the body. Actually, all three of the just-mentioned topics are so interrelated that we cannot consider any one of them in detail without necessarily considering the other two.

Reception of the body of Christ in the Holy Eucharist is not the only reason we have for first directing our attention toward the role of the body in human life, however; our discussion in the first chapter of the relationship of Christianity to reality urges us to make the same beginning.

We have already indicated that the acceptance of reality belongs to Christianity's essence. It is instructive to notice how we described reality's acceptance and the

terms we used to express reality's first dimension. We said
that the "real" belongs and that we know in our bones that
we belong if we are real. We spoke of the effect of imprisonment on a person's life and of the commitment a person
makes when he takes off in an airplane; we talked about
the type of reality a plague has and the effect of self-inflicted tattoos. Christians were said to embody the answer
to the world's problems, and we took notice of how convincing the reality of the evolving material universe is to
us, noting that our reality is a constituent feature of that
evolution. "Bones," "imprisonment," "airplane rides,"
"physical sickness," "tattoos," "material universe," "embodiment," all refer to the type of reality we know
through our bodies.

We have been saying that it is important to "face reality." When we talk to a child, we say, "Face me." Both of
these expressions would be impossible if we were not, in
some fashion, bodies. It is hard to see how any discussion
of man could begin more appropriately than with an
analysis of that aspect of his being.

We are in the world through our bodies. No one dis-
putes that statement; the simple facts of conception and
birth furnish all the proof we need. Most people count
their time in the world from the semiautonomous existence they received in a hospital's delivery room on the
day of their birth. They were there to be delivered, something that would have been quite unnecessary if they
were not a body!

As universal as the acknowledgment is that we enter
the world because we are bodies, most people do not realize the implications of their admission. The fact seems so

obvious that they are kept from understanding the implications of their own words. We must ask ourselves, accordingly, "How are we related to our bodies and how are we in the world through them?"

The careful reader will have noticed that in references to the body already made I have spoken of our being a body instead of our having a body. The role of the body in our lives together with the differences between *being* and *having* are themes which Gabriel Marcel was the first to explicate convincingly for our day. There is a sense in which we both are a body and have a body, as we shall see, but contemporary thought has gone a long way toward establishing the priority of the body we are over the body we have.

Paradoxical as it might sound at first, we most obviously are our bodies when we pay the least attention to them, when, in other words, we live through them and go beyond them.

Sitting down to a good dinner, for example, I say, "I'm starved." My stomach may be empty, but *I*, not it, am the one who is starved. During the meal it is *my* enjoyment of the steak that I savor, not my stomach's; I am immediately involved in an I-it relationship, thank goodness, for it is with the immediacy of the "I" that I enjoy the *it*.

When a hiker stands on a bluff looking at the plain beneath him, he lives in the scene; he is glad to be alive, glad to see. He is so much his body, and through it so much in the world, that he does not think about his body as a foreign thing at all. A skier is outside of himself through the tingle of his face, the gripping of his ski poles, and the flexing of his knees. Getting a breath of fresh air after having been cooped up in a smoke-filled room or inhaling deeply on a spring day are ways we thankfully live beyond ourselves through our lungs. By getting spring air into *us*, we live outside of ourselves in nature's spring; we are refreshed by nature as a part of it. At such times, feeling most ourselves, we are not conscious of our rib cage the way we are when we are afraid we have cracked a rib and are trying to point to the source of our discomfort in a doctor's office.

Our bodies are "most me" when we transcend them. When we bump someone in a crowd and turn around to apologize, suddenly discovering that the person we hit is an old friend whom we have not seen in years, our joy in seeing him flows through our body as we spontaneously reach for his hand. At such moments handshakes are prolonged, not quickly dropped. Personal warmth is naturally the physical warmth of bodily contact.

We do live through our bodies; we do transcend them. But how is that possible? How can we understand the fact? If the body is only a "thing" like other things in the world, if we as persons are somehow outside of our bodies, using them merely as external vehicles of expression, we are left with a problem indeed.

A first step in understanding our relation to our bodies is the realization that we can be said to transcend something only by passing through it, not by having nothing to do with it. Bypassing something, in the sense of "leaving it out," is the work of abstraction, not transcendence. We speak of living through our bodies, and so of transcending them, but if the body is only a thing externally related to us, how, we must ask ourselves, can we get into it to pick it up? How can we grasp it to make it useful to us? I can

grasp a hammer with no difficulty because I grasp it with
my hand, but our present question is of quite a different
order; we are asking now how we can grasp our body
before it is our body. What could "grasping" even mean in
such a situation? The concept "grasping" proceeds from
bodily experience and is quite meaningless apart from
it.

We are confronted here with the "mind-body problem"
which baffled (and beat) Descartes in the seventeenth
century and which has continued to baffle (and beat)
everyone who has followed Descartes' method of analysis
through the present century. Jacques Maritain gave the
ultimate summary of Descartes' position years ago when
he said that the best Descartes' analysis of man could
come up with was an angel driving a machine. If the body
is an extended thing and the soul an unextended spirit,
each complete in itself, they can never be brought together in a genuine unity. With such a view, we will never
be able to understand our most immediate experience in
the world. We need to embrace but one friend to give the
lie to such a theory.

If the body is a mere thing, it is so different from me, so
external to me, that I can never live through it. We can
think of wind passing through a screen, but actually, in so
doing, the wind is escaping the screen rather than passing
through it. Wind does not take the being of the screen
up into itself in order to transcend it; wind passes through
the screen in virtue of being so external to it that its nature is unaffected by the screen. But human life, as we
shall try to show, is not unaffected by the fact that we are
bodies.

If I as a subject am pure spirit and the body is only an

object, there is a sense in which I can say that the body exists for me (that is, over against me, before me), but then the body can never *be me*. If we are not our bodies, however, the whole approach to reality expressed in the last chapter should be unconvincing. If I am only a spirit, I cannot be in space, which means that I as a person have no location; but if that is the case, how can a slap on the cheek bring a hysterical person back to "himself"?

Our immediate experience of ourselves testifies that we are not just in space through the body but that we actually live space through the body. We live both space and time in our most intimate personal lives; we are not in space the way a figure is on a piece of paper, nor are we in time the way an island is in a river that constantly flows past it. Early in the morning, late at night, or after we have been sitting in a cramped position for a while, we luxuriate in the spatiality we *are* when we stretch and turn our trunks, extend and stiffen our arms and legs, and let out a loud yawn. A person with good posture is not just more attractive from the outside; he is actually able to be more himself in the inmost depths of his being. We cannot help but "stand up" for what we believe (which is why Christians stand for the Creed), and it is natural to shrink away and try to become small when we have been less than ourselves.

We are not dimensionless points scattered through the world; a person is an extended place. The posture and breathing exercises experts in relaxation teach businessmen are not gimmicks unworthy of human beings; we are in the world through our bodies, and the way they are our bodies influences the way we are in the world (something

we will have more to say about later). Things get out of
hand if a person makes his body an end in itself, if he is
only concerned about his breathing, pulse, and posture;
but we cannot be ourselves apart from our breathing,
pulse, and posture, as the universal fear of death testifies.

The expression "I could dance for joy" reveals something essential about us. When do we use it? When we are
pleased, overjoyed, fulfilled, most completely ourselves.
We become so much ourselves that we cannot contain
ourselves; still we must be ourselves, and we exclaim that
we could jump with delight. Dancing in its most spontaneous form could well be called the celebration of our
spatiality. Erwin Straus has pointed out the different significance space assumes for us when we walk and when
we dance.[1]

In walking, we pass through space; we dance, however,
within it, even trying to expand our spatiality. In the
dance, the trunk of our bodies becomes much more active
than it does in walking; it assumes angles and attitudes
that deviate appreciably from our usual posture in facing
the world. In the normal purposefulness of our lives, we
pass through space to get from here to there, from one
place to another; to deviate from the straightest path or to
have to step backward is contrary to our intention and
threatening to our purpose. In the spontaneous expression
of the dance, on the other hand, stepping backward, lean-
ing over, swinging obliquely, do not threaten our purposes; instead, they are a delightful manifestation of our
life.

[1] Erwin W. Straus, *Phenomenological Psychology*, trans. by Erling Eng
(New York: Basic Books, Inc., 1966), pp. 22 f.

Movement in the dance tries to fill and express space rather than pass through it or overcome it. At least at the dancing moment we know that the structure of space is an essential ingredient of our lives, and we show how at home we are in space by filling as many dimensions of it as we can. We do not limit the expression of ourselves to a restricted form of locomotion; in the dance, as we said, we do not want to get someplace else, we simply want to be as completely present as possible. The completeness of our presence is shown by our free movement through as many spatial dimensions as possible. We are ourselves when we move backward, forward, sideways, up and down, and in combinations of all these. King David dancing before the ark was being himself in his joy.

We *are* space in our bodies before we have any thoughts about being *in* it through our bodies. The spatiality of our lives lies at the root of Marcel's seminal contention that the body is the "type" of the world. By that he meant that the type of relationship we can have with our body determines the type of relationship we can have with the world. The point is, the body as a thing—as something in space before me—is not my most immediate body. It is derivative.

Traditional thought knew the body was special, but it described the body as a special type of *thing*, one, for example, that we cannot get outside of. The body is always something we are looking out from. But such specialness is not special enough to account for all of our experience; we are in something we cannot get out of when we are trapped in an elevator or when we are strapped in a straitjacket. Our relation to our bodies is so special that it cannot be adequately described in "thing terms" at all.

Instead of the relationship between things being able to explain the relationship we have with our bodies, close examination will reveal that it is only because of the unique relation we have with our bodies that we can have relationships with things. As Maurice Merleau-Ponty pointed out, we are able to understand such a statement as "The book is on the table" only to the extent that we are able to think of ourselves as either the book or the table and then derivatively apply to one or the other the categories which fit the relationship of external objects to our bodies.[2] Only because I know what it means for something to be on me do I know what it means for a book to be on a table.

My body cannot simply be one thing among others in the world, for it is the *mediator* of all the things in the world to me. In its mediatorial role, the body is the *source* of all our knowledge of things and so must be qualitatively different from them. No one would deny that the body, at least to some extent, can become an object for us. But even when it is an object, our body has a dimension which things lack. The "double sensations" which the body is able to have furnish us with a good illustration.

When my right hand touches my left, I am aware of it as a "physical thing." But at the same moment, if I wish, an extraordinary event takes place: here is my left hand as well starting to perceive my right. . . . The physical thing becomes

2 M. Merleau-Ponty, *Phenomenology of Perception,* trans. by Colin Smith (New York: The Humanities Press, 1962), p. 101.

animate. Or, more precisely, it remains what it was . . . but an exploratory power comes to rest upon or dwell in it. Thus I touch myself touching; my body accomplishes "a sort of reflection." In it, through it, there is not just the unidirectional relationship of the one who perceives to what he perceives. The relationship is reversed, the touched hand becomes the touching hand, and I am obliged to say that the sense of touch here is diffused into the body—that the body is a "perceiving thing," a "subject-object."[3]

My two hands grasping each other can become alternately—and, in a sense, even at the same time—subject and object for the other, a possibility we have with no other object in the world and a fact which differentiates my body from all other objects in the world.

The body as the source of our relationship with all the things of the world, instead of being a prison which confines us, is actually a means by which we transcend ourselves. In the sense that the body is I, it is such transcendence. Recognized as an aspect of our lived existence, the body is just as obviously a carrying of ourselves beyond ourselves, as our bodies, in turn, are carried by something beyond themselves when we ride in an aircraft. The reference beyond ourselves we cannot escape noticing in an airplane ride is possible only because of the reference beyond itself which the body is, for it is only through our bodies that we recognize and have our dependence on the aircraft.

An additional consequence of our embodiment, greatly

[3] M. Merleau-Ponty, *Signs,* trans. by Richard C. McCleary (Evanston: Northwestern University Press, 1964), p. 166.

stressed today, is the fact that a human being is always in
a *situation*, never merely in a position. Dolls can be put in
positions that are no more than positions, but that is not
the case with human persons. Every position of a human
being is at the same time an aspect of a situation which
exceeds it in depth and dimensions. Newspapers in Great
Britain which list job-wanted advertisements under the
heading "Situations Wanted" are perhaps unwittingly
closer to human reality than American papers which head
such columns "Positions Wanted."

Let us look more deeply into the difference between
being in a position and being in a situation. The spatial
position of a thing can be described completely in terms
of external coordinates. We can completely determine the
position of a spot on a piece of paper by measuring its
distance from the sides of the paper. Nothing pertinent to
the location of the spot is omitted by such an analysis. If
we are drawing a graph and want to designate a certain
point as "zero," we can locate that point anywhere we
wish. Considered simply as a location on a two-dimensional plane surface, no position is intrinsically different
from any other position. One position will do as well as
another, and there is nothing to keep us from arbitrarily
substituting one for another if we wish. After all, a point
is a point.

In itself no point is different from any other point, but
is man's body no more than a point that can be completely
defined in external terms? Not according to our most immediate experience of ourselves. We have seen that our
bodies somehow *are* our lives. My lived body is not a
thing which can be exhausted by geometrical description.

That is the reason why I am always in a situation rather than just being in a position. We may say that a pretty woman is a "doll," but her place, as Ibsen knew, is not in "a doll's house": she is a human being who situates herself, not a toy to be positioned by someone else.

The space of our immediate lives is the space of *action*, instead of the space of mathematical abstraction.

Our human life-space is not a mere geometric spread in which there are no directions, and all points are alike. It is oriented into a forward and back, right and left, up and down with respect to the different places and directions towards which the body is able to move. The future is what I face with my body ahead of me, before me. As I move ahead towards this future, I am passing by things, and what I have *passed by* lies behind me in *the past*. So long as I maintain the delicate balance between the forces that threaten to upset me, I can make my own way, freely and with poise, toward the things that are coming, and for which I may be prepared. When I lose my poise, my movements become awkward or backward, and I lose control over the situation. In such backward or awkward movement I cannot foresee the things that are coming, but know them only after I have passed them. I no longer face the future, and my knowledge, like that of a detached spectator, is restricted to what I have already passed by in the past.[4]

A person situated in the world is someone for whom everything that happens has a special meaning. Events in our lives cannot be arbitrarily substituted for one another

[4] John Wild, "Husserl's Life-World and the Lived Body," in *Phenomenology: Pure and Applied*, ed. by Erwin W. Straus, (Pittsburgh: Duquesne University Press, 1964), p. 23.

the way "point zero" can be on a graph, because, as we
have seen, our lives are not empty extensions of undifferentiated space. Our lives are identifications with space
which force us to *be* a point of view instead of just being a
point to be viewed. We can be only one place at a time,
and we must look out on the world from that place even
though we would prefer a different perspective. The body-
we-are-as-subjects is the directly lived organizing center
of the world of each one of us; our lived body is a meaningful structure of relations necessarily making us a center
of a world instead of merely allowing us to be located in
space.[5]

Our lived experience of our bodies is different from our
external, spatial knowledge of them. A student of mine
illustrated the point when he told of playing a game with
some friends. The game involved a mirror into which one
was supposed to look as he traced diagrams on a piece of
paper. Trying to control his hand by means of the external
information supplied by the mirror turned out to be very
difficult. The trick, the student discovered, was not to ex-
ternalize himself at all; he found that by living his body
from the inside and paying as little attention to the image
in the mirror as possible, he was able to trace the figures
much more easily.

As I actually live my body, its location and the location
of its parts are primarily determined by the tasks in which
I am engaged in the world. Sitting at the desk writing, my
attention is focused on my hand, on the way I am pres-

[5] A clear and valuable integration of the general position we are presently
discussing can be found in Alphonse de Waelhens, *La philosophie et
les expériences naturelles* (The Hague: Martinus Nijhoff, 1961), *passim*.

ently disposing of myself through it. All the other parts of my body are immediately located for me in relation to my writing; all the regions of my body "fall into place" through my project of the moment. The task of writing locates all of my body with such interior sureness that there is not the least necessity for my looking at myself as an external observer would, charting, for example, the location of my legs by their position relative to my chair, my desk, and the floor.

So it is, too, in enjoying a breath of spring air or shaking hands with a friend. The action of greeting my friend through my hand locates all of my body in a friendly situation; I need no spatial diagram to know where I am. Our activities in the world give us an "undivided possession" of our bodies which is totally foreign to the external knowledge we have of them as extended substances whose "parts exist outside of parts"—the classical definition of physical matter.

Our bodies are unified and our worlds are defined by the tasks we initiate in our lives. A biologist looking through his microscope, an astronomer aiming his radio telescope, the painter at his easel, the housewife choosing food at the store, her children running up and down the aisles, the baby playing with his blocks—all illustrate the essential interrelation between body, task, and world. The world of the children in the grocery store is not the world of the astronomer; the activity each performs is a source that defines his world. World, body, and task enter into the constitution of each other, and none can be itself by itself. Our body is our rudimentary situation in the world. Its very being refers beyond itself, and so it is at the same time both an activity for us and a vehicle of our activities in the world. To be able to see the body as *task*, as relationship, and not just as a *thing* which is externally related to us, is one of the most important insights for religion and its relation to the world that is available to us.

Through the characteristics of our body which enable us to relate to it as an object, we have continuity with all the objects in the material universe. We are thus afforded a means of incorporating that universe into our personal lives by extending to it the style we creatively live through our body-as-subject. Through our bodily lives we can thus incorporate the whole universe into the pattern of our self-expression. In that way our personal body can become as inclusive as the totality of our lives in the world; our "individual body" can become, as it has been put, a "*universal body*."[6]

We do not yet control as much of the physical universe as we would like, but our control of it is growing, and through that growth the means of our self-expression is expanding. But even the parts of nature we cannot control solicit our reactions to them; the ways we respond to disaster and sickness, for example, are still ways we meaningfully express ourselves in the world and so spread the style of our lived bodies.

A correlate to the truth that, taken into my affirmative life, the universe becomes my body, is the fact that the way a person lives in his body indicates the way he lives in the world.[7] The attitude a person takes toward his

---

[6] Jacques Sarano, *The Meaning of the Body*, trans. by James H. Farley (Philadelphia: The Westminster Press, 1966), p. 139.

[7] *Ibid.*, pp. 141 f.

body is indicative of the attitude he takes toward the world. Psychosomatic medicine has emphasized the necessary relationship we have to the world through our bodies. Even a person ignorant of such medicine recognizes that he normally reveals the type of person he is through his relationships with other people and through his actions in the world. There are people, however, who for one reason or another withdraw from such open expression of themselves; they try to conceal themselves in their public lives. But because no person can be himself without some expression in a world, the style of living of such people necessarily seeks expression in some other milieu. That milieu, it has been suggested, is found in the body itself. Here the body becomes the substitute for the world instead of our gateway to the world.

Dr. Medard Boss contends that the symptoms of hysterical and organ-neurotic patients can be best understood if the symptoms are analyzed from the point of view of a relationship toward the world which has retreated into the body of the patient for its expression.[8] Ulcers and hysterical gestures never tell just about the body of the patient; they always indicate something about the patient's whole manner of living. There is much information to suggest that people bring on their illnesses, and Humbolt's statement that "a man dies of his character" has increased in acceptance over the years. Illness is frequently an escape from reality, but such an escape can only be to another reality—that of the sickness itself. We may escape from one world, but we can only escape to

---

[8] Medard Boss, *Psychoanalysis and Daseinanalysis*, trans. by Ludwig B. Lefebre (New York: Basic Books, Inc., 1963), pp. 143 ff.

another world—and any world we can get into will be related to our body.

Realizing the relationship of our lived bodies to our lives in the world may help us understand why many people who want to change the way they live in the world are often so helpless. Because they want to change—or have God change—their lives, they feel that they must employ resolutions and prayers which are big enough immediately to include their whole lives. So people pray, "O God, make my life better," or they make a general resolution to "be different." But if we have seen anything in this chapter, it is that we are not in the world in a general way; we are always in the world in a specific situation through our lived bodies. Our general problems in the world must be attacked at their specific source, and frequently that is the body. If I change the way I worry about my body, for example, I will *be* changing the way the whole world can worry me. To spend less time looking at my hair in the mirror *is* to be more affirmative in the world!

If one quits caring for his body as if it were a thing, he will immediately find himself living in the world beyond the body. Here there is no middle term: we either try to use the body as a source of isolation or we are at once involved beyond ourselves—the way the lungs of the person taking a deep breath of spring air relate him to the rebirth of nature around him. As a matter of fact, the body can never become a perfect source of isolation even if we want it to, for as long as we live we know we are vulnerable to external attack through our bodies. They are always related to something beyond themselves.

"Meeting others" is a problem many people have; they tighten up and become defensive, are ill at ease, and feel threatened at social gatherings. But the insights we have been discussing should help us see that relationship to other people is actually a dimension of our bodies. We cannot escape other people for the simple reason that we cannot escape our bodies: our bodies are at the same time us *and* relation to them. To recognize the relational structure of the lived body can thus become a means of overcoming the strangeness of others, which is a primary source of their threat to us. To be sure, the bodily relationship we have to others is a rudimentary relationship when taken just in itself, but that does not stop it from being the source of all right relationships.

Nothing would help our age lose its title of the Age of Anxiety as quickly as feeling at home in our bodies. The anxiety of modern man appears to be nothing less than an anxiety about being in the world: he feels alienated in the world, but he cannot escape it. Does not his world problem show itself, just as we would expect, in his relationship to his body? Few things sell better today than books about relaxation and peace. We have already referred to exercises for tired businessmen so they can learn to relax. To be at one with the body is the way to be at one with the world; by making our bodies foreign objects, we make the world a foreign object and consequently feel at home in neither of them. The world is always different from us and in that sense polar to us, but it need not be strange to us if, just as in our dealings with persons, we treat the world as the kind of thing our bodies are. If we do that, the world will be in us and we will at the same time transcend it. We would then realize the Christian goal of being "in the world but not of the world."

Understanding how basically we are in the world through our bodies will also help us not only tolerate, but justly advocate, differences among men. Pluralism is the condition of human society because we cannot be disassociated from our embodiment. A person who takes the located nature of his embodiment seriously cannot reasonably expect himself to be everything; once he accepts the fact that he can only be one point of view and quits trying surreptitiously to be everything at once, he will rejoice at, instead of being jealous of, the abilities of others.

The body in *haute couture* is the place of style. There are women who spend almost all of their time "fixing themselves up." Such a woman works upon her body as an object and hopes for nothing more out of life than to be a devastating object when she is displayed in public. There are movie stars in Hollywood who are so beside themselves in their concern for their bodies as objects that they have made it possible always to be beside themselves by covering all four walls of their bedrooms with mirrors.

Instead of being an object to be styled, one's personal body *is* his style of living. To admit that our bodies differ from one another in this sense is to admit that our styles of living differ from one another. In one swoop, then, we can see the necessity for cultivating style in our own lives and not expecting everyone to have the same style in his life.

The world-informed-by-our-style-of-living, the ex-panded body we make as persons in the world, is com-pounded bit by bit through the innumerable choices we make every day of our lives. That world grows as part of us if we positively affirm ourselves in it, or it becomes an increasingly strange place of threatening objects to us if we shrink from it.

The body as agent of our location in the world requires us to make choices. We cannot be everywhere at once and we cannot be everything at once. Forcing us to choose between alternatives, the body is the source of human ethics and the reason why every man has some kind of ethic. We have to choose our mates, friends, leisure activities; we have to choose the way we will work, play, spend our money. Choices are necessary if we are going to be our-selves, and being ourselves necessitates choices. We fre-quently rebel against that fact; we often prefer not to commit ourselves. But if the chairman of a meeting finds a whole group of people trying such evasive tactics, a vote by a show of hands will clarify the issue. Because of our bodies, even to refuse to vote is to stand in some definite place. No matter what we may wish, because of our body's necessary location someplace, the body's mere presence *is* commitment.

More than just forcing us to choose, however, the body illustrates in itself, and in the world of which it is the nucleus, the choices we have made. We have seen the sense in which our body-worlds result from choice. Un-mentioned until now is the further fact that the nature of our body-world can also illustrate another's choice for us: that is the necessary point for understanding Christian redemption in Christ.

God in Christ overcomes the world in the sense of creating a new world through the body of Christ. Life in Christ is a gift, something we do not deserve, which is the reason for saying that the Christian life is one of *grace*. By freely coming to us in his only-begotten Son, the Father is telling us that he has *chosen us* to become something more than we are.

God does not ram anything down our throats, even our salvation. Although he freely comes to us in Christ and chooses us because of his love for us rather than for our merit, the completion of our redemption depends upon the way we respond to him. The world we make through our lived bodies depends upon our choice, but in Christianity that choice becomes an answer to a question originating beyond us. The proper choice of Christians is *consent* to growth, consent to radical newness. It is a leaving of self, such leaving as is actually life in a new world.

Christianity is centrifugal; it works in the world from the inside outward, as we noted in the last chapter. Rooting our worlds in the world seated in Christ's body, Christ becomes a force within us proceeding through and beyond us like the centrifugal force moving through water in a pail we swing around us at arm's length. Christianity is a force moving through us rather than from us; that force is God's choice—love—of us. God comes to us in his incarnate Son so that we can know his presence with us from the ground up, that is, through the body outward, where our being in the world originates.

We should now begin to realize with new depth the degree of God's love for us in Christ. The centrifugal force of Christianity in our lives results from the centripetal force of God's love for us in becoming incarnate! He loves us with a thoroughness we can only describe as embodiment—Incarnation. But because of that, he begins to make his world through us at the first level at which we make our worlds for ourselves. Christianity is not a new suit of clothes for an old man; it can be nothing less than a rebirth because in it we enter a new world, God's world in Christ.

In the Incarnation each one of us has the love of God given to him in the same mode of being in which he lives his own life. Thus we need not fear to be ourselves in the world. That is God's guarantee of our being—again, as we also mentioned in the last chapter. God's love passing through us by his choice of us—that is, by his coming to us as an *embodied* Son—gives us the ultimate assurance we need to be expanding body-subjects in the world instead of shrinking body-objects.

Christian love, because it is Christ, must be lived through our bodies; the role of the body in our lives is, in fact, the key to our redemption in Christ. As deep as our involvement in our lived body is, so deep is Christ's victory in the world. Christianity is a bodily fact, not an abstract hypothesis. The Easter victory means that the constancy of our body-sense (of coenesthesis) and the persistence of the world the body exposes us to are the constancy of Christ's love for us. We can show *his* victory only by affirmatively embracing in his Spirit the totality of events to which the body opens us. We lead Christian lives by letting nothing in the stream of our experience daunt us. To hesitate in the face of reality or to refuse any opportunity to be creative in the face of danger is to fail to accept the victory of the Word made *flesh*.

To be a Christian means to let the reality of Christ's body answer the needs of our bodily involvement in the world, instead of trying to change our lives by abstract theories about ultimate reality.

III ✤ In the Face of Christ

"What's in a face?" we ask. There are two answers: Nothing. Everything.

Nothing is in a face if we mean the face as a *thing*. We teach our children not to judge by appearances, and in our better moments we try not to judge by them ourselves. We know the tragedies which result when we form opinions about people based solely upon the way they look. A person's face can keep us from him—if we try to reduce him to the thing we call his facial surface.

"He only married a pretty face" is as total a condemnation as can be made of a woman. It does not say much for the man either. Psychologists have taught us that a pretty face may actually work to a woman's detriment, preventing her from developing normally as a person. A father may be so intimidated by the pretty face of his daughter that he is afraid to treat her normally or to discipline her as he should. We frequently read too much into faces. We think that a wide-eyed person must be honest, for such eyes are the way we usually picture innocence. We think handsome people must be good.

St. Paul wrote: "For it is the God who said, 'Let light

shine out of darkness,' who has shone in our hearts to give the light of the knowledge of the glory of God in the face of Christ" (II Corinthians 4:6).

Can we picture the face of Christ?

Did he have blond hair? Salvador Dali thought so when he painted "The Sacrament of the Last Supper." Was Christ bearded or clean-shaven? Did he have a thin or full face? What about his forehead and chin? What kind of nose, lips, and complexion did he have?

All of these questions miss the point of seeing the glory of God in the face of Christ. The questions betray nothing more than a curious concern with external appearance. They only go "skin-deep," and that is not deep enough to help us with our deep problems—the problems that get under our skin.

What is in a face? Everything, in the sense that every person has a face. "Men without faces" are men without identity, which makes them less than men. Above all, to see a person in his face is to know him in experience, in a living situation, not before it.

When we are interested in someone, we look him in the eye, in the face, because that is where *he* is. Imagine an upset, desperate person begging for help. He is apt to be too much in his face; he may be so intensely there with his problem that we have to fight to keep from turning away from him. "Wait until I see him face to face; then I'll be able to deal with him," cries the person who feels betrayed. What he says is true, for when the other person is there with his face, a full confrontation will be possible. A lover looking into the face of his sweetheart sees all of her there. Is it not significant that when lovers exchange pictures, they almost invariably exchange portraits of their faces?

To see God in the face of Christ is not to see the contour of a face as much as it is to see life in a face; it is to see the glory of God in the world. As the Greek word for *glory* is used in the New Testament, the "glory of God" means the mysterious mode of being which is God himself; that glory is often compared to *light*, as in I Timothy 6:15-16 when God is described as "the King of kings and Lord of lords, who alone has immortality and dwells in unapproachable light, whom no man has ever seen or can see." The blinding glory of the unapproachable God himself is said by Paul to be seen in the life of Christ.

We will be far afield if we worry about the shape of Christ's nose and chin. Seeing God in the face of Christ is to see character expressed in a face; it is to see openness, concern, and love in a life. Seeing the crucifixion and resurrection of Christ are the seeing of his face; "Christ's face" is a structure of living originating in his physical body but far transcending it. The character in his face is the offer to change "the face of the world" to such an extent that nothing less than a new world results.

A principal message of St. Paul is that the body of Christ—the face of Christ—is still in the world. That body is the Church, the People of God, whom Paul at one time in his life vigorously persecuted. When the glorified Christ appeared to Paul on the road to Damascus he asked, "Saul, Saul, why do you persecute me?" (Acts 9:4; cf. Matthew 25:35 ff.). The revelation given to Paul at that time was the strict nature of the identity of those who believe in Christ with Christ himself.

The relationship of believers to their Lord is so intimate that Paul could think of no better way of describing them than as members of Christ's body. "For by one Spirit we were all baptized into one body. . . . Now you are the body of Christ and individually members of it" (I Corinthians 12:13, 27). In Romans 12:5, St. Paul writes: "We, though many, are one body in Christ, and individually members one of another." Within the body we are all one (Galatians 3:28). Christians "live no longer for themselves" (II Corinthians 5:15); they "walk in love, as Christ loved us and gave himself up for us" (Ephesians 5:2).

Having become members of Christ's body in baptism, Christians, through the indwelling of the Spirit, are to live in their bodily lives the life Christ lived, and still lives, in his glorified body. A Christian's "spiritual worship" is to present his *body* "as a living sacrifice, holy and acceptable to God" (Romans 12:1).

Wherever Paul's letters were known in the Christian world, the Church was referred to as the body of Christ. That description of the Church is one of the longest unbroken threads of Christian tradition; but, as the centuries separated later believers from the culture within which Paul lived and spoke, while his words remained, their full meaning was lost. Christians have never ceased to speak of Christ's glorified body in heaven, of his body the Church, and of his body in the Eucharist; but it is safe to say that, by the time of our century, the overwhelming majority of Christians thought of that terminology as little more than a gratuitous inheritance from the past. It was a historic metaphor accepted in the name of orthodoxy (if orthodoxy was still desired), but to many it suggested little more than "another one of those problems" Christians are saddled with.

Due to apparently independent lines of research—New Testament study on the one hand, and contemporary studies of the nature of man on the other—St. Paul's terminology can now take on new plausibility and meaning for us. Thanks to biblical investigations, we can realize more adequately what St. Paul meant by his words; and thanks to recent descriptions of the nature of man, we now have an independently established beachhead on ground common both to St. Paul and to our day. We are presently equipped to assimilate some of his most basic insights without compromising our own, an indication that we may be approaching a new fullness of time after what no one will deny have been some lean years.

"Man does not *have* a body, he *is* a body." "The body is the soul in its outward form." These statements might well have been made by one of the philosophers or psychologists whose views were examined in the last chapter. Actually, however, the statements were made by two biblical scholars, Bishop John A. T. Robinson and J. Pedersen.[1] The remarks occur in the course of Bishop Robinson's discussion of the meaning of "body" in the thought of St. Paul. The Bishop, Fellow and Dean of Clare College, Cambridge, at the time he wrote the words quoted, points out that in St. Paul's writings "flesh" (*sarx*) and "body" (*soma*) stand for the common Hebrew word *basar*, which, in turn, meant primarily man's body as *flesh*.

[1] John A. T. Robinson, *The Body: A Study in Pauline Theology*, Studies in Biblical Theology, No. 5 (London: SCM Press, Ltd., 1952), p. 14.

The most important thing for us to understand in the interest of historical accuracy is that the Jews of biblical times always considered man to be a unified whole; they did not think that his soul could be separated from his body (even though they may have referred to him from time to time only in terms of his bodily parts), and they thought of his body (*basar*) as the basis of his communal solidarity rather than of his individualistic isolation. In both of the last two characteristics, the Jewish concept differed radically from Greek thought.

A significant insight for our understanding of St. Paul is that he, too, as a Jew of his day, always considered man to be an unbreakable whole, even when he referred to man by only one aspect of his being. Thus when Paul uses the word "flesh" (*sarx*), he does not mean man's flesh as it is separate from or opposed to man's spirit; he means the whole man approached through the unmistakable concreteness of his physical being. In his physical being man is continuous with the earth and consequently different from God. Because identity with earth is at once contrast with God, St. Paul often referred to man as "flesh" (*sarx*) in order to contrast man in his sinfulness to God in his righteousness.

Still, in St. Paul's eyes, there was nothing in itself sinful about man's material existence in the world; sin arose only when man preferred the world to God. After all, it was God's creative preference which put man in the world in the first place. Because, to Paul's wholistic way of thinking, man could only be himself in his body, but because "flesh" (*sarx*) was the way Paul sometimes described man in his sinfulness, Paul had to have another way to describe man in his wholeness when he lived for God instead of for the world. That word was *soma;* although we translate it "body," it means man's whole life, including everything meant by "flesh," but with that life directed toward God instead of toward the world.

The Church is understood by St. Paul to be the body of Christ with all the distinctness of the concept *soma.* As *body,* the Church is radically identified with a historical person, Jesus Christ in the flesh; the material concreteness of Paul's use of "body" will not allow the Church to be thought of as a merely social body (as we speak of a group of people forming a "body of people"). The Church as *body* in Pauline thought refers specifically to Christ's physical being.

Even if St. Paul's use of "body" were recognized for what in fact it was (which has not always been the case), if we had nothing more to go on than that, his message might seem sterile and foreign to us today. If we think of the materiality of man's body as that body is an object, it is something which separates him from all other men and which is too opaque for anyone else to participate in. Under such circumstances, being made members of Christ's body in baptism would seem to be too much of a job even for the Holy Spirit. There would also be problems about the reception of Christ's body in the Holy Eucharist. In fact, that problem was found in New Testament times, as we see in St. John's Gospel. "The Jews then disputed among themselves, saying, 'How can this man give us his flesh to eat?' So Jesus said to them, 'Truly, truly, I say to you, unless you eat the flesh of the Son of man and drink his blood, you have no life in you; he who eats my flesh and drinks my blood has eternal life, and I will raise him up at the last day. For my flesh is food indeed, and my blood is drink indeed. He who eats my flesh and drinks my blood abides in me, and I in him' " (John 6:52-56). The word translated as "body" in this passage is *sarx*, "flesh." There is little wonder that "many of his disciples, when they heard it, said 'This is a hard saying; who can listen to it?' " (John 6:60).

Now, however, we can understand a sense in which man's materiality is not impersonal and opaque at all; it is actually a source of subjectivity and illumination. Not the least of its illuminating benefits may be the light it throws on biblical theology! Upon evidence that has arisen quite independently of St. Paul in particular and biblical thought in general, we can now understand that man's body is a dimension of his subjectivity; it is immediately he as he is a person. A person's body is not just an object before him that is different from him like the car he drives. As he is his lived body, his corporeality is not closed, opaque, and the source of isolation; instead, it is open, clarifying, and his necessary presence in the world with other people. The lived body is a transcending pattern of life necessarily carrying him beyond himself in himself, making other people and the world constitutive of his most intimate being. It is therefore with good reason that the ancient Jews could consider the body as the principle of communal solidarity rather than the source of personal isolation. They did not come to that conclusion because of their philosophical sophistication; they lived more spontaneously than that. They simply lived their body-as-subject instead of letting their body confine them as an external object.

I am not saying that Paul's concept of the body is pre-

cisely the same as the contemporary position presented in
the last chapter, but I am saying that the two views are
compatible and reinforce each other. Each refers to a
body that is more than and different from the externally
observed body. Modern thought can help us see in new
detail how Paul's contentions are possible.

Being incorporated into the body of Christ makes sense
if we think of that body in terms of the lived structure we
have discovered our personal bodies to be. Our incorporation into the Church is our incorporation into the basic
structure of Christ's life. The incorporation is not spiritual
in a way that would deny its materiality. As we have seen,
Paul used the term "body" precisely because of its mate-
rialistic meaning and the concrete identification it forces
with the Word made *flesh*. The human body, we have also
seen, is always spatial and material in nature; but it is
lived space, expressive matter. We can be incorporated
into Christ's body only in our bodies, for only in them can
the type of structure which is Christ's body find its kind of
being in us.

Christianity begins in our bodies as we live through
them the integrating structure Christ expresses through
his body. We must stress the fact that Christianity begins
in the body; it is not something outside the body or beside
the body. We need a *thick* Christianity if *we* are to be
Christians; we need something with body to it (ours!)
that can be unmistakable and effective in the world.
Christianity needs body—something that can be seen for
what it is in itself. As it is, our Christianity is often so
thin that people have no trouble "seeing through it" and
discovering at its core only our wishful but uncommitted

selves. A religion that makes us a member of Christ's body is different from one that is only a projection of our unredeemed need for security.

The belief of Christians is that Christ the Savior continues to live in his body because of the resurrection. Only a body can be resurrected, and Christianity's tenacious insistence upon the reality of the resurrection has been at the same time its insistence upon the necessity of the body for man. Without Easter, without resurrection, there would not have been, and there never can be, true Christianity. History itself is possible only because of the type of life man lives in his body. Nothing is more reasonable, therefore, than God's remaking of history through the body of his Son. The primacy of history and the primacy of the lived body in our lives go together.

The good news of Christianity is that when we are incorporated into the body of Christ by baptism, we share the life he lives in his resurrected body. We are incorporated into the most basic structure of his ongoing life. Upon entering the Lord's resurrected body in baptism, we enter a new order of bodies, which constitutes the redemption of the world.[2] Through that order the Father realizes "his purpose which he set forth in Christ as a plan for the fulness of time, to unite all things in him, things in heaven and things on earth" (Ephesians 1:9).

It is likewise the body of the resurrected Lord that Christians receive in the Holy Eucharist. "Proclaiming the Lord's death" to the world is a manner of living Christ's resurrected life. It is only in the strength of that life, pos-

[2] Cf. John A. T. Robinson, *On Being the Church in the World* (London: SCM Press, Ltd., 1960), pp. 40 ff.

sessed by the Spirit of life, that we can die to the world in the Christian sense of living to God. We saw in the last chapter that the lived body is not to be identified with our external bodily image. We live our body-as-subject in too immediate a way for it to be equated with our external, reflected appearance. The nature of our body as a pattern of living, accordingly, helps us understand how Christ's glorified body in heaven, his mystical body the Church, and his sacramental body in the Holy Eucharist can be essentially one. They are different manifestations of one pattern of living; their external appearance was never intended to be the means of their identification.

The reference we have just made to Christ's glorified body in heaven should, perhaps, have a brief word of explanation before we go on. Many people think that such talk is too naïve for our day. I do not agree with them. To say that Christ's body is now in heaven certainly makes heaven a place, but it does not require that heaven be a place within this universe.

Location, we have seen, is a necessary feature of every human person; such location is what calling heaven a place is all about. Actually, the idea is most compatible with the insights we have developed: as our bodies are the basis for our understanding of geometrical space (there is, remember, a sense in which we *are* space before we can talk about being *in* it), so Christ's glorified body is the basis for our understanding the type of location heaven has. We have our priorities wrong if we wonder where the empty space is that Christ's glorified body fills; his lived body determines the characteristics of his present location in heaven just as our bodies determine the type of location we can have on earth. To say that Christ still has a body is to say that he is still a self that centers a world. To add that his body is *glorified* is to say that his present life, due to the creative intervention of God, exists in a dimension of reality that transcends the dimensions of our present being.

Such perfection does not destroy the significance of heaven as a place, but it does make that place unlocatable within the limited dimensions of the physical universe. Since, upon adequate analysis, God's creative power is the only sufficient reason for the type of location we now have, there is no contradiction involved in his creating new dimensions of being for us in the glorification of his incarnate Son. Since we completely depend upon God for what we already are, there should be no barrier on our side to acknowledging that he can perfect our being in the future in ways we do not know about now. If there is a God, our imagination is not the key to his power.

Let us turn now to a more detailed consideration of the Holy Eucharist. In instituting the eucharistic sacrament, Christ himself proclaimed, ". . . this is my body . . . this is my blood . . ." (Mark 14:22-24; Matthew 26:26 ff.; Luke 22:19 f.; I Corinthians 11:24 f.). By feeding on the eucharistic body within the mystical body, the Church, Christians are enabled to live no longer for themselves, "for as often as you eat this bread and drink the cup, you proclaim the Lord's death until he comes" (I Corinthians 11:26). Christ dies for others. Christians are nourished by the very blood which was "poured out for many" so that they may completely give themselves for others.

It is the love of God for man which is uniquely shown

in Christ and made available to us through the sacramental body and blood of Christ. Was not Christ's love
expressed in his body? Love is shown by willingness to die
for one's friends. "Greater love has no man than this, that
a man lay down his life for his friends" (John 15:13). "By
this we know love, that he laid down his life for us; and
we ought to lay down our lives for the brethren" (I John
3:16). Love is the means by which Christ's mystical body,
the Church, grows; and that love is offered to us in the
Eucharist. Being fed by Christ's body within his body, we
are able to accomplish our work as different "members" of
his body should, namely, in a way which "makes bodily
growth and upbuilds" the body "in love" (cf. Ephesians
4:15 f.).

Since, as baptized Christians, we live in Christ's body
through the nourishment of the body and are meant to
present our own bodies as living sacrifices to God, it
should be no surprise that St. Paul was able to say, "The
body is . . . for the Lord, and the Lord for the body" (I
Corinthians 6:13). St. Paul is referring to man's life in the
flesh, the life of his most immediate feeling and inclination, the life that is so constant and usual that some have
thought it too common to have any religious significance
at all. Paul's point was that it is precisely the *common*
aspects of life that do have religious significance. Our
bodies, not our separate souls, "are members of Christ" (I
Corinthians 6:15).

Our Lord's shocking statement "This is my body" was
not made in a vacuum. It was not a chance remark
dropped in a casual conversation; it was something said at
a definite time with deliberate intent in the midst of an

action which had been carefully prepared. The words were spoken at the meal in the upper room to help explain and define the action which was in process at the moment. The words did not refer to something that was spiritual, timeless, and totally removed from the movement of the present; instead, they helped define a personal activity going on at that place and time but which could not be confined to the room or the hour in which it was going on. The action then being accomplished extended throughout (and therefore still continues in) Christ's whole incarnate life: it was the giving of himself for others.

A meal takes time and involves the type of personal participation out of which the history of the world is made. It is because of that fact that the meal in the upper room was able to be made a unique participation in the ongoing historical life of Jesus. The action of the meal, instituted as an event within the life of our Lord, was a participation in the action of his life transcending the meal, and it is that fact which gives the meal its full meaning. Because of the freely willed pattern of living in which Christ took up and extended his "individual body," he, through the active incorporation of the bread and wine into that life-structure, enabled them essentially to participate in what was, at the time, the still-future giving of his body on Calvary. By identifying the bread and wine with his body and blood, Christ made available to man in a new mode the giving of his body for the world on the cross. All of us shape the present by what we intend to do in the future; in the institution of the Holy Eucharist, Christ's future actually defined his then-present gift to his disciples.

The identification of the supper in the upper room with the culmination of Christ's sacrificial life on Calvary was effected by the sameness of Christ's will in those two events. In each case he gave himself in a singleness of will for others; that is why, as it has been said, the upper room anticipates Calvary and Calvary guarantees the upper room. To use contemporary terms, Christ's "project" (or "task") is the basis of identity between the upper room and Calvary.

It would have once been thought sufficient to say that our bodies are the means by which we carry out our tasks, but if the position taken in the last chapter is correct, that statement is wrong: our bodies *are* tasks. There can be tasks only within a world, and the body is our being-in-the-world. As we live creatively, we have seen, our style of living incorporates more and more of the world into our extended personal body. With that background, we can understand that the integrating project of Christ's life, his revelation of the will of the Father, defines his body. As our projects determine the nature of our worlds by shaping and enlightening the only reality we know, so Christ's project of revealing the will of the Father creatively defined the nature of the bread and wine at the Last Supper. It is a full, historical definition, one which permeates the existence of the elements Christ was working with, and one which can do the same thing to our existence if we will make it our project to be used in his project. But nothing less than a body answering a body, our whole world answering his whole world, will do.

By saying, "*This* is my body," as he distributed the previously blessed bread to his disciples, Jesus indicated the identity which had been effected between the structure of his life and the being of the physical bread by his use of it. He instituted his continued eucharistic presence among his people, in other words, with the same physical concreteness that the Incarnation itself required. Because he is specifically *located* for us in the Holy Eucharist, he expects us to be similarly located for him in our lives in the world. We must be clearly identifiable. He becomes recurrently present for us through our participation in the ongoing activity he began in his body; through that participation he expects us to be extensions of his presence in the history we make through our bodies. Through the particularity involved in identifying himself with *certain* bread and wine which has been defined by a *certain* activity, he tells us that his life in the world is a *certain* perspective on the world which differs from other perspectives. By being in one place rather than another, a characteristic of every human body, he thus precipitates our choice. We must either be with him for what he is or we cannot be with him at all: we must be with him in a way that can be located. The eucharistic presence of Christ thus epitomizes the nature of our personal commitment to him and is meant to supply the structure of our whole lives.

That Christ chose food as the means of effecting his presence with his disciples is highly significant. No activity is more immediately related to our bodies than the eating and assimilation of food. We sometimes talk about "food for thought," and there is even a magazine called *Reader's Digest*, but the primacy of material food for the extended uses of the word "food" is obvious. Christ is himself only as an embodied person, but his purpose is not to remain external to us the way our physical bodies force us to be outside of each other in geometrical space. Christ is external to us and outside of us in the sense that he is God incarnate come to us. The very concepts of love and dialogue require a reciprocity among persons that is possible only if the persons are distinct from each other. By coming to us, Jesus Christ necessarily confronts us: he confronts us with the love and judgment of God. God is different from us, and the recognition of that fact is the first degree of our knowledge of him. But the love of God in Christ confronts us only so that his identity can be established for the giving of himself to us. No more adequate an indication of the situation could be found at the bodily level at which it must begin than the "confrontation" we have with food before we eat it and the identity we have with it after we have eaten. Once having given himself to us through his appropriation of bread and wine, our physical assimilation of the eucharistic food is the sign of our personal assimilation by Christ.

The eucharistic body of Christ—which must certainly be his lived body—is uniquely fitted to involve every dimension of our lives. The eucharistic consecration of the bread and wine is the work of the Holy Spirit; because Christ's lived body is the presence of the Spirit in the world ("the Lord is the Spirit" [II Corinthians 3:17]), the Holy Eucharist can suitably structure our "spiritual lives." On the other hand, the presence of Christ in the Holy Eucharist is such a completely personal presence that it has material consequences, too. It can be itself only when it shows in our visible lives. Actually, of course, our spiritual and physical lives cannot be separated.

The sacrament of the Holy Eucharist was instituted in the midst of the continuing historical dialogue between God and his people Israel. The dialogue involved Abraham and Adam and reached a culmination in Jesus Christ who was at the same time both God and Israel, caller and called. Word and community played vital roles in the dialogue of which we are speaking, and we shall turn to a consideration of them shortly; for the present we must notice some final characteristics of the role of the body in the Eucharist.

The eucharistic activity is an extension and consummation of the historic activity of God's chosen people. It is by the action of the New Israel, Christ Jesus himself, that the eucharistic bread and wine are taken up into and identified with the Savior's bodily presence in the world. The Eucharist as the key to Christian living can never be understood if the activity of the Eucharist is isolated from the continuous activity of the People of God in the world.

We can find additional meaning in the Eucharist if we follow up in still more detail the parallel between our Christian lives in the body of Christ and our lives in our own bodies. God the Father in his creative might has made us embodied persons and then called us to new life in the body of his Son. What could be more "natural" for man? God, who wills us to be embodied persons in the first place, has taken up the body of Christ into his same creative will and made that life-structure available to us in the Church and in the Holy Eucharist. In our lives in the world, we have seen, there is a sense in which we willfully take up our bodies in order to extend them outward into the universe. Such a "taking up" of his body in order to extend it is the structure of man's natural, embodied being. How much more creatively that structure can be employed by God!

In the Holy Eucharist, God's will, working through the historical activity inaugurated by the Son and now continued by the Church, incorporates physical food and drink into the life-pattern of the Son, the pattern that once centered in his natural body and is now centered in his glorified body. Having so identified the food with the lived structure of Christ's body through the mystical body's ongoing historical activity, the Person who is the Source of both the food and the body creatively identifies us anew with Christ through our participation in the consecrating activity and by our eating of the consecrated elements. Willing to come to the Lord's Supper is to will to do what Christ did—and does. In everything Christian, our wills must answer God's will before we can benefit from his gifts; but even granting such cooperative response to God's will, our identification with Christ's body in the Eucharist is too immediate completely to be willed by us. Let us examine in more detail what that means.

I am suggesting that no person can will to receive Christ's eucharistic body and blood with nothing more to go on than his will alone. By the same token, no one can absolutely will his own body either; in our daily lives we are able to take up our bodies "into" our wills and perfect our bodies by extending them in the universe only because we are our bodies before we will to extend them. The situation is similar in our Christian lives. Before we can will to "take up" Christ's body in the Holy Eucharist, before we can so completely cooperate with the action of his body, we must somehow already be his body. Just as in our natural lives we must be our body before we can

will our body, so in Christianity we must be Christ's body
in a primordial sense before we can will the extension of
that body in a mature, ongoing sense.

We can be helped by these considerations better to understand how the eucharistic body perfects the mystical
body, the Church.[3] The eucharistic bread and the Church
are both the body of Christ; yet the first is truly the perfection of the second, for the consecrating activity we perform in the Eucharist, which is meant by Christ to extend
to the whole universe, is analogous to the willful taking
up of our lived bodies in our natural lives and perfecting
them by extending our pattern of living in them to the
whole world. In our Christian lives we are meant to take
up the structure of the body into which we were born at
baptism and willfully use it to consecrate to God the
whole world we define by our activities and projects.

We can also see now, from an experiential point of
view, why Christianity's initiatory rite of baptism must
necessarily precede the covenanted mode of participation
in the Holy Eucharist: even in our natural lives we must
be our bodies before we can perfect them.

Everything we have said about life in the body of Christ
and the eucharistic activity which is its perfection indicates that life in Christ cannot be adequately conceived as
if it were but one fact in an abstract land of facts. It
cannot properly be so conceived even if that abstract land
is called "theology"! Christianity is a concrete, situated
way of living in a concrete, historical world. The first
thing we must say about it, we saw, is that it has the same

[3] It is an interesting historical note that the Church was first called the
"mystical body" as it actually participated in the Holy Mysteries, the
Eucharist.

type of reality as the most immediate world in which we live. The true meaning of the Eucharist can be discovered only at the level of its historical institution by the Christ at a precise time and place in the world of men, which is to say that the Eucharist is a way of existing which we can comprehend only through the way we exist.

We cannot be Christian and try to live in ourselves by ourselves. Because we are our bodies, we *are* an outside; we are not pure centers of consciousness with no location in the world who can completely know themselves from within themselves. Jesus Christ still exists in us and in the world through his mystical body and through his sacramental body. As we are incorporated into his body in our bodies, both our lives and his are necessarily turned toward the world. That is why we cannot be Christians without making a world, without making a Christian cosmos. That is why our eucharistic activity is a cosmic activity.

The translators of the New English Bible were closer to the truth than they may have realized when they translated the sixth chapter of St. John's Gospel. After quoting Jesus' remark to which we earlier referred, "In truth, in very truth I tell you, unless you eat the flesh of the Son of Man and drink his blood you can have no life in you," the translators continued, "Many of his disciples on hearing it exclaimed, 'This is more than we can stomach!'" (John 6:53, 61). To eat the body of Christ *is* more than we can stomach; his body is more than we can contain! Once he is within us, he transcends us, carrying us beyond ourselves in the centrifugal manner we have already described.

St. Paul was a good illustration of such living. Writing

of his ministry to the Corinthians, he said: "We are afflicted in every way, but not crushed; perplexed, but not driven to despair; persecuted, but not forsaken; struck down, but not destroyed; always carrying in the body the death of Jesus, so that the life of Jesus may also be manifested in our bodies" (II Corinthians 4:8-10). All the mercy and comfort we receive from the Father in Christ Jesus is given to us only so that it may overflow us for the consolation and comfort of others (cf. II Corinthians 1:3-6).

St. Paul's life was a eucharistic life, and so ours is meant to be. Once admitted into the structure of Christ's body at baptism, everything we willfully do through our bodies is our participation in his eucharistic body. To sleep, to eat, to accept interruption, to be concerned, to be patient, to be honest, to be available, to be cheerful, to be humble, to be compassionate, to *be*, is to "eucharistize."

The continuing action of the Eucharist is nothing less than the face of Christ in the world today.

IV ✤ There's a Word for It

"Oh, what's it called? You know; there's a word for it."

Such a plight is especially human. We have all experienced it. We do have words for things, and neither we nor our world are themselves until we can find the right words to express them.

Things have a place in our world by having a name. One of the first things we do with children is name them; some people even name their children before having them. At any rate, offspring take their place in our families by being named. Naming, too, has a lot to do with the way certain people treat their pets as if they were children. If someone remembers my name after a prolonged absence or after only a casual meeting, I feel good because I know by that fact that I have a place in his world.

As we mentioned in the Introduction, expression through language is the most unique and powerful ingredient in human culture. We are inserted into reality through language much as we are through our bodies. Just as we have seen that we become more ourselves by expanding the pattern of our lived bodies outward into the universe, so we become more ourselves as we communicate with one another through speech. Speaking and language are, in fact, the primary means by which our personal expansion in the universe takes place. Language is a way we handle things; it is a means of dealing with things in a certain way. It enables us to be creative and active in the world. We have only to think of the increasing power man has gained in nature by means of the language systems we call physics, chemistry, and engineering to be convinced that language is not accidental to human destiny or to the world in which we live. It is not too much to say that words make our worlds. There is a world of physics, a world of chemistry, a world of engineering; those worlds are defined by the modes of expression used by physicists, chemists, and engineers. "Publish or perish" may not always be a good slogan for faculty promotions in our universities, but "communicate or perish" is a condition of human existence. The purpose of education is to equip one with the vocabulary necessary to enter as a full participant into the special worlds of man. The purpose of education is communication.

Language is the vehicle of culture and has been called the richest gift society gives to a child. The anthropologist Edward T. Hall wrote a book a few years ago entitled *The Silent Language;*[1] the book was very successful and even became required reading for people who were sent to overseas posts by the United States Government. Professor Hall's contention was that many of the most important things we communicate to other people are communicated in the nonverbal or silent language of behavior. Be-

[1] Greenwich, Conn.: Fawcett Publications, Inc., 1961.

cause too many Americans who go to foreign countries pay attention only to the words that are spoken or printed in those countries, the Americans frequently miss, and so unintentionally frustrate, the personal dialogue their new acquaintances are trying to have with them. Communication actually takes place at many levels and in many different ways. Professor Hall contends that culture *is* communication and that culture can be best understood on a linguistic model. Developing the consequences of his position, he maintains that cultural situations should be taught like language. He then goes on to analyze culture as he would a language in terms of isolates (which are compared to sounds), sets (which are compared to words), and patterns (which are compared to grammar and syntax). Teaching cultural situations in that manner, the claim is made, such vague factors as "empathy" can be done away with in anthropological work.

If culture is communication and if communication can be of many different types, it will be helpful to see how early communication begins in human life and the different forms it takes. To begin our investigation of its first appearance with the period of life we call infancy seems reasonable enough, but such a beginning has added significance if we realize that the word "infant" in its Latin roots means "someone who does not speak." Children were first called infants because they did not speak with words. No one doubts nowadays, however, that children communicate long before they speak; learning a language merely enables them to do something better that they have been doing for some time.

Professor John Macmurray states:

In the human infant . . . the impulse to communication is his sole adaptation to the world into which he is born. Implicit and unconscious it may be, yet it is sufficient to constitute the mother-child relation as the basic form of human existence, as a personal mutuality, as a "You and I" with a common life. For this reason the infant is born a person and not an animal. All his subsequent experience, all the habits he forms and the skills he acquires fall within this framework, and are fitted to it. Thus human experience is, in principle, shared experience . . .

This original reference to the other is of a definitive importance. It is the germ of rationality. For the character that distinguishes rational from non-rational experience, in all the expressions of reason, is its reference to the Other-than-myself. What we call "objectivity" is one expression of this—the conscious reference of an idea to an object. But it is to be noted that this is not the primary expression of reason. What is primary, even in respect of reflective thought—is the reference to the other *person*.[2]

There is a lot in those two paragraphs that we must go into further as this chapter develops. But first let us examine the importance of communication and speech in human life where that importance has been emphasized by an abnormal deficiency. Dr. Bruno Bettelheim, Director of the Orthogenic School at the University of Chicago, has had a long career in dealing with autistic, withdrawn children. His observations on the roles of communication and language in such children are most instructive.[3]

[2] John Macmurray, *Persons in Relation* (New York: Harper & Row, 1961), pp. 60 f.
[3] Cf. *The Empty Fortress: Infantile Autism and the Birth of Self* (New York: The Free Press, 1967), *passim*.

Our own contention is that man's vocation is to express himself. Expression is his way of being in the world; and that expression, fully developed, is the way he makes his world. It is amazing how early such expression starts.

According to Dr. Bettelheim, an infant is much more active in his relation to the world than we commonly suppose. We should not think that an infant is merely passive in his satisfactions, and we do him an additional injustice if we think of his response to the world—when such response occurs—as nothing more than instinctual behavior. An infant is active in his nursing, for example, carrying on what can only be described as a monumental task in his limited world. No wonder that such a task exhausts him and that he sleeps a lot! He expresses himself, however, not just in sucking, but in the way he responds to the position in which he is held, how tightly he is held, the way he is picked up, etc.

In the autistic children with whom Dr. Bettelheim has worked, it was not the absence of passive satisfactions which caused their difficulties; instead, it was the lack of positive response other people made to their personal expression. Mutuality, a need expressed and satisfied on the part of all participants in an activity (mother and child in the case of an infant) is the crux of all truly personal relations. Where mutuality is lacking, personal development cannot continue.

Aware that an outer world exists which answers his needs, that he can influence that world through signs such as crying and kicking and pulling, but that the world does not always respond to him, an infant, through the lack of such response, is taught his first lesson about the advantages of mutuality and cooperation with others. Thus, within the communication with his mother made possible by the language of his bodily movements and of his vocal signals, the infant can have a truly *human* experience, that is, one that humanizes him—an experience of mutual, responsive involvement with another person.

Simply to have someone care for our physical needs and being able ourselves to act in our environment does not furnish a sufficient basis for fully human development, according to Dr. Bettelheim. To such physical service as may be received and such actions as may be taken must be added an appropriate personal response to the expression of our feelings. To have no response or to meet a constantly inappropriate one discourages a child from expressing himself at all. In time he ceases to bother with self-expression and may even regress to a state of sensitivity and apparent cognition lower than that of some infants.

The human responsiveness upon which our personal development depends is first made possible by the language of our bodily movements and the often ambiguous signals, such as crying, which we have so far discussed. With the appearance of spoken language, personal dialogue can proceed almost without limit. When vague signals are perfected by spoken words that can have precise meanings, the richness of our communication and our personal being grows in direct proportion. Even at the earliest age, however, Dr. Bettelheim suggests, vocal communication of the mother with the infant through humming, singing, and talking helps to achieve the security in human life that, for example, clinging to its mother produces in baby monkeys.

To indicate how speaking is continuous with and perfects experiences which first proceed through a child's body, we may note a report of one formerly autistic child who said that in his present life he was able to derive— from talking with his friends about his feelings—the "very same comfort" he had first experienced when he had been fed baby food by members of the staff in his dormitory at the Orthogenic School in Chicago.

There is no doubt that language and speech are ways we *confirm* ourselves, *commit* ourselves, and *involve* ourselves with others.

Let us first consider the role of language in self-confirmation. Only at the level of language can the "I," the center of all my relations with others, be fully distinguished from "you."[4] Language is the means of overcoming solipsism, for to say "I" means that I am able to distinguish myself from *you*, and within that distinction I tacitly recognize our "togetherness" in a community of responsible agents. One autistic child, when she first began to experience herself as a person in a real relationship with another person, manifested the new world in which she lived by saying intermittently during the day nothing more than "I" and "I'm."[5]

On the other hand, if a person receives no acknowledgment of himself from others, or if he receives the constantly frustrating acknowledgment of opposition or nonconcern, he often gives up language altogether. There are instances in which such a person will develop a secret, idiosyncratic language; but if his feelings of trauma and isolation are deep enough, he may become totally mute. As his life becomes less and less personally involved with

[4] *Ibid.,* p. 56.
[5] *Ibid.,* p. 209.

others, his condition is reflected in his language, which becomes more and more abstract and impersonal. Language and the world in which one lives are correlative. Autistic children who feel alone in the world omit personal pronouns when they speak. Someone hearing them talk for the first time may think they are mentally retarded and not quite rational, but actually such a limitation of language makes very good sense to the person who is using it. Omitting personal pronouns such as "you," "we," "us," "they" in a world which is experienced as having no people is quite reasonable.

The use of language is also a way we commit ourselves, as can be seen by the linguistic restrictions employed by autistic children who want to avoid commitment in the world. Psychologists have identified in children a desire for language, a tendency to speak, which precedes even the first expression of phonetic forms. That desire to be oneself in language is partially incarnated in the emotional and expressive tone with which a person normally speaks —the way he identifies himself with his language. Such identification has its origin in the infant's expressive babble.

Autistic children, however, frequently speak in a flat, monotonous, undifferentiated tone. In addition to being mechanical and unhuman in their intonation, they are often adept at repeating arbitrary lists of words and names. Once more we must not think of such behavior in terms of mental capacity or limitation; it is, rather, a mark of the essential correlation of language with personality. A child who refuses to use the pronoun "I" will nevertheless commit long lists to memory because the repetition of such lists involves no commitment to the world and makes no revelation about oneself to others the way using "I" does.

Because language is a way we are involved with others, it can be used to test the degree of others' involvement with us. Here again, autistic children furnish us with a "telling example" (an interesting idiom in itself). When such children talk, they frequently speak in riddles; but here, too, their manner of communication makes very good sense in their world. Speaking in riddles is a way they can linguistically protect themselves and at the same time test the extent of another person's involvement with them by seeing how concerned the other person is to figure out what they are actually trying to communicate.[6]

Having given some indication of the importance of language and speaking in our lives, let us now begin to analyze their nature in more detail, so that we can better understand the importance which has so far been pointed up only descriptively.

We have seen that human beings express themselves from the period of infancy onward, and we have suggested that such expression is nothing less than their vocation in the world.

Animals express themselves, too, communicating warnings, anger, the desire to mate, excitement, and fear to one another. Impressive as such communication often is, we must not confuse it with human speech. An animal is bound to the totality of the situation in which it lives and to the presence of its organic needs in a way that man is not. Animals can express their feelings and give signals to one another, but they cannot set off aspects of reality the

[6] *Ibid.*, p. 430.

way human beings can or refer to one such aspect at a time to the exclusion of other aspects. Some animals can even make elementary generalizations, but those generalizations are severely limited by the concrete circumstances in which they occur. Another way of putting all this is to say that man can *objectify* meaning in a manner animals cannot.

The inability to objectify, that is to say, the inability to set something apart and recognize it in itself for itself (i.e., apart from our organic needs), even keeps animals from imitating man in the true sense of imitation. Visitors flock to the gorilla cages of our major zoos and stand spellbound as the man-like animal looks them in the eye, scratches himself, and sometimes repeats their gestures. But such repetition on a gorilla's part is not imitation; it is a sympathetic entering into a concrete situation, rather than an understanding of what imitation is and then a performance of it for its own sake. Animals, in other words, cannot objectively recognize a piece of behavior for what it is and then initiate it in a responsible way as their intimate response to us.

Authentic language indicates the intervention of a *person* in a situation, as Georges Gusdorf says.[7] By such intervention experience becomes a "universe of discourse," a field of infinite possibilities instead of a closed situation. The experience of a human being is different from the experience of an animal because human experience can be talked about. In that sense, the human world is par excellence the world of speech.

The time has now come to be still more precise in our

[7] Georges Gusdorf, *Speaking*, trans. by Paul T. Brockelman (Evanston: Northwestern University Press, 1965), p. 36.

own use of language. We have frequently used "speech" and "language" together, but the two are not the same. Language is something speech uses. Ferdinand de Saussure said that "language is speech less speaking," by which he meant that language is a certain static network of formal relations.[8] Language is a series of differentiations which are able to be themselves only within their total system. Everything in language is its full self only in contrast to other elements; the signs employed in a language are constituted by their difference from all the other signs of the system. We explain words through their relations with other words, the method we are familiar with in all of our dictionaries. None of the signs used in language have their signification in themselves alone; they are all constituted by their opposition and relation to other signs. We learn language from within it, not from outside of it.

Language is also communal. It is its complete self only within a community and is never completely possessed by a given speaker. Speaking, on the other hand, is always the act of a concrete subject and so has an individuation and efficacy that language, because it is only a static system of signs, lacks. Languages change, but they change because of the speakers who use them, not because of themselves.

Considered just as a system of signs, language is ambiguous; it can be used a number of different ways for a number of different purposes. I can use the word "four"

[8] Ferdinand de Saussure, *Course in General Linguistics*, ed. by Bally and Sechehaye, trans. by Wade Baskin (New York: Philosophical Library, 1959), p. 77.

to number persons, elephants, books, automobiles, ideas, trees, houses, errors, victories, planets, or an indefinite number of other subjects. The speaker who uses language is always an "I," and words have their real meaning not as they are listed in a dictionary but as they are used by a speaker to mean one thing rather than another, as they are used to overcome ambiguities found both in dictionaries and in our living experience. Words are most themselves when they are used by a speaker vividly to make present something beyond themselves. Here another similarity between words and our bodies is discovered: each is most ours when it permits something else to hold our attention. If words get in our way when we are trying to express ourselves, they are not *our* words and so not good words.

Because of the relation of a speaker to language and because the purpose of language is to reveal the speaker or some aspect of reality the speaker especially intends, language can never be fully understood apart from the subject who uses it. Language is much more a style of living than it is an abstract grammar or syntax. Taking students into a mode of personal living, we now know, is the best way to teach them a language. French or German can be best learned in a French or German home. Learning tables of conjugations and declensions may keep us from learning a language for what *it* is. We *are* expression, and language is our most complete mode of it. We learn to speak because other people cannot help speaking to us, and we are ourselves only in answering them.

More distinctions and shades of meaning can be made through language than through any other activity of man.

Language, as spoken, is a form of life for people; it is *they*, not just a vehicle they use. Edward Hall's identification of culture with communication is a good insight, but when he premised that cultural situations could be learned without empathy—without distinct reference to the subjects who speak—he was maintaining that language has an independence from speakers which it actually does not have.

There is truth to the contention that language is as immediately present to us as our bodies. We can be ourselves only in our bodies and we can be ourselves only in speaking. But if that is the case, we can know language only in its use; it cannot be studied in abstraction from the subjectivity of the people who use it. The present tense of a language is the moment *I* am speaking, and every person who has spoken in the history of the world has spoken in what had to be the present for him. That means, as Merleau-Ponty has pointed out, that an understanding of the human present, its creativity, its special orientation towards the future and past, its contingency and perspective, becomes the unique key to everything spoken in the historical past. The past is not the adequate key to the present. Here again, Professor Hall's contention that cultural situations can be taught in terms of isolates, sets, and patterns alone seems wide of the mark.

"Word" rather than "speaking" or "language" was mentioned in the title of this chapter, and, although there is an obvious connection between all three, we must now pay special attention to "word" as such. Once we have done that, we will go on briefly to consider the nature of signification and meaning; we will conclude by showing the centrality of linguistic meaning to human life as that centrality can be illustrated by the methodology of psychoanalysis.

Man, we have seen, is an embodied subject; he is not a bare soul or an unincarnate spirit driving a machine. A consequence of that fact is that man's "mind" can contain no purely spiritual, completely unembodied thought. As we are ourselves only in our bodies, so our thought is itself only in words. Speaking is a way we indicate and acknowledge meaning in the world. Meaning exists for a child before he develops the power of verbal speech, but so genuine is his expression before his mastry of words that psychologists such as Dr. Bettelheim are forced to describe the infant's preverbal behavior in terms of "body language." Our bodies themselves are words, ways we express ourselves. Even such a nontechnical news magazine as *Time*, when reporting the story of a man who climbed out on the ledge of a tall building and squatted there poised to jump, once noted that the postured body was a tremendous effort at communication. In authentic speaking, our words are animated with the same life as our body itself.

Our words are actually an extension of our embodied life, but once the meaning we intend to express takes verbal form, we have a freedom of expression that far exceeds our bodily ability alone. There are many types and levels of meaning in our lives, but language, through the employment of words, is the only type which can treat all other types. By means of words we can talk about painting and music, but we cannot paint music or musically score a painting. We cannot use painting to step back from itself and examine a painting, but language is so agile that it can even examine itself. There is language about language. Self-examination is another difference that separates man from the lower animals, and the ability of language to be turned upon itself shows again how man can be himself only through it.

By referring to nonverbal types of meaning through words, we make those meanings communicable in a new way. So it is that men are able to cooperate with one another and reinforce one another in all the areas of their lives. To recognize that language can refer to every aspect of man's life is not to claim, however, that it can exhaust or adequately substitute for the different forms of meaning we experience. An essay about Beethoven's violin concerto will never replace the concerto itself, but language can help us better understand the concerto we hear and lead others to listen to it. Language is also necessary if the conductor, soloist, and orchestra are to have a successful rehearsal and reach a common understanding of how the music is to be played.

Language is our primary means of communicating with one another. Language, in any form, involves reference to another, for language is the means we use to *signify* something. Signification may be defined as the negation of "for myself alone."[9] What do we really mean, for example, when we say that something—a sunset, a chair, or a tree —has meaning in itself? When we say of something that *it* has meaning, are we not saying that *everyone* can recognize the meaning? The "in itself" of a thing's meaning is

[9] Alphonse de Waelhens, *La philosophie et les expériences naturelles.* (The Hague: Martinus Nijhoff, 1961), p. 125 ff.

actually fixed by the fact that, in speaking of it, our act of signification makes that aspect of the thing available to everyone. Such reference is possible because significance places a distance between a person (the speaker) and that to which he refers. To be able to separate himself from what is present to him while it is present to him is the way man transcends every situation in which he finds himself. It is nothing less than the ability to speak.

Animals are limited in the situations in which they find themselves, as we noted earlier in this chapter; man, on the other hand, while being in one situation, can look at it from many different points of view. He can consider it from different "angles" because he is a true subject, which is to say that he is someone who is able to stand over against that which confronts him, thereby enabling that other thing to be viewed as an object in itself.

Man's power of objectivity qualifies everything he does; it enables him to speak, and it enables him to live in a distinctively human world. Meaning arises in a situation only where an action is more than its factual existence, where, in other words, signification is possible. A handshake is meaningful in a distinctively human way because it is not simply a "pressing of flesh," as a recent slang expression puts it, but is a sign of the kind of relationship we call friendship. Similarly, a kiss means love to lovers and the word "integer" means a certain formal nature to a mathematician.

The way man transcends things even while remaining in their presence makes not only our language but even our sense perception of the world different from that of the lower animals. All the bodily movements we employ in sense perception (those of our hands, eyes, and whole bodies) are gestures we initiate toward the world which make the world peculiarly *ours* rather than the world of a dog, cat, mouse, fish, horse, or frog. The mobility we embody forces our world to be one of perspective; we cannot see everything at once, and we can see the same thing from different points of view at different times. Just a moment ago we remarked that man can see the same thing from different angles. As soon as we realize that our world depends upon perspectives, however, we must admit that our world is communal. "Perspective" means "partial," and "partial" implies that other perspectives of other people exist at the same time I am aware of my own perspective. The perspectival nature of our bodily insertion into the world qualifies all of the special acts of sensing and thinking that we can abstractly consider and later build into our cybernated machines.

It is the absence of such a fundamental style of living at the bodily level that keeps machines from being human. Machines can perform and integrate certain intellectual operations and even intensify the sensual discernment of man, but those operations are not vitalized and unified from within by the felt oneness of a lived body. They do not take place within the life-world such a body makes possible. It is not our thought patterns, but their world setting and their context of destiny, that differentiate us from machines.

The type of perspective we derive from our lived bodies roots us in a common, communal world. The complicated perspectives of the world we develop through our words in the special sciences simply carry on our human style of existing in highly restricted areas. Every special word-style develops within a general life-field structured by our body. It is our bodily orientation which supplies our lives with the peculiarly human dimensions of decision and history. Every fully human word embodies those same dimensions; that is why only an incarnate Word can make us truly human!

Professor de Waelhens sums up the relationship that exists between a subject, the world, and other people as neatly as possible when he points out that "object" and "for others" are constituted by one and the same process. An object, by definition, is something that is separated from a subject; and that separation, in itself, is availability to others. To be a subject who uses words, then, is to be at once in a world which essentially relates one to other people. Words detach meanings from individual experience and so make those meanings available to the experience of others.

We have been emphasizing the close relationship that exists between our lives and language. That relationship is so close that our bodies have been called words, and we have seen that our words are themselves marks of our bodily insertion into reality. All of that being the case, it should come as no surprise to us that our being as persons is presently described as "semantic," that is, something which needs interpretation. One type of such interpretation is supplied by psychoanalysis, and the success of psychoanalytic therapy has been well described, under the circumstances, as a "talking cure."

Near the beginning of this chapter we observed the linguistic difficulties of autistic children. Our analysis of language should now have shown us how we can and why we must relate to others through words. All discourse is essentially related to other persons, and Professor de Waelhens has suggested that a sick person can be differentiated from a healthy one precisely to the extent that he does not truly speak to *another*.[10] A sick person's discourse is blocked upon itself, thereby keeping him from others instead of revealing him to others. That was the exact use of language made by children in Dr. Bettelheim's school. Psychotherapy has been described as an attempt to re-establish authentic discourse addressed to another in the life of a person who has lost such openness.

A typical therapy session is an isolated, protected period of time within which a client can express himself to his therapist without fear of hostile consequences. It is an area in which a person's actual history is suspended as much as possible and in which he develops a new history through his primarily verbal communication with another person. Past events are talked about, but in the talking about them, they are interpreted and integrated into a present interpersonal relationship. Even though the past seems to be the primary concern in many therapy sessions, it is never precisely *the* past of childhood or adolescence, for, as we have seen, a speaker can only speak in the present. The past recalled in conversation with another person is the past qualified by the present. The past recalled in the presence of another is a present means of relating to the other. In time, a new history which the client can completely assume, the one developed through the intersubjective use of language with the therapist,

[10] *Ibid.*, p. 152, fn. 3.

hopefully appears. Since that history is an ongoing one in the present, the client becomes increasingly himself in the present and finally no longer needs the protection of a professional therapy session in which to be himself.[11] A talking cure!

It is not too much to say, in conclusion, that language is the way man lives in the world. Nothing more encompassing can be said about anything. Language differentiates, and the world is a complex differentiation; language objectifies, and the world stands over against us as an object; language enables us to communicate with one another, and the world we are in is always communal.

Not to try to express oneself as clearly as possible is to try to deny the nature of life in the only world we know. Both expression and the world take effort; both make claims upon us. We are always in dialogue. The fact of our incarnation prevents us from being mere observers of anything.

The separation of language from the immediacy of reality gives language a type of externality and makes it somewhat ambiguous when considered in itself alone, but those marks also enable it to be a field for man's freedom. Externality and ambiguity hurl a challenge at our creativity rather than giving us an excuse for indolence. A human being cannot be himself without language; thus his responsibility does not extend to whether he will speak or not. By existing we speak. Our responsibility as human beings is to search for the right word both to express our-

---

[11] *Ibid.*, p. 155. Cf. Paul Ricoeur, *De l'interprétation: Essai sur Freud* (Paris: Editions du Seuil, 1965), especially Books I and III.

selves and to understand the universe. To be ourselves, we must constantly become more than ourselves; we do that as we express, through the creative speaking which is our lives, more of reality than we have expressed before.

We must "live in God's world, the real world, which is still in the making." The words we use are a most important means of doing that. They are so important that God has sent his Word to be their source. We will talk about that in the next chapter.

V ❖ The Last Word

We always try to have the last word. In arguments we feel the last word is important because words are the way we state our positions; and our positions, in turn, are so important that we frequently argue about them. We have seen the sense in which a person is a position. Does not the sureness with which we state our opinions reside basically in that fact? I am truly a person; I am a position; therefore, my word states the true position on this matter! The syllogism is not logically sound, but it does describe the way many people debate.

Men of wit almost always have the last word in a conversation. By so doing they are in charge of the situation, either dismissing it or controlling it in a way which shows their superiority. Perhaps no time in a child's life is more trying to his parents than that in which he "acts smart" and has an answer for everything.

An adolescent's desire to joke and get the last word in is a sign that he is growing up; it shows that he is beginning to feel personal equality with his parents and desires to transcend his early dependence upon them by sharing his gratuitous remarks with them. There is a good deal of bravado and testing in teen-age humor, but that, too, is necessary for personal growth.

To get the last word in is a means by which we as persons prevail in events. Jesus Christ has been called the last word of God; Christians confess that that Word is the way God has chosen to prevail in the world. The idea is taken from the beginning of the Epistle to the Hebrews: "In many and various ways God spoke of old to our fathers by the prophets; but in these last days he has spoken to us by a Son, whom he appointed the heir of all things, through whom also he created the world. He reflects the glory of God and bears the very stamp of his nature, upholding the universe by his word of power" (1:1-3).

The passage maintains that God has spoken to man before Jesus Christ in the prophets, but that God has spoken in a special and final way in his Son. The identification of person with word is implicit here, although, as we shall see, that identification is more explicitly made in other parts of the New Testament.

We have mentioned that a person is seen in his face. For the Jews a person could be seen just as completely in his word. Word and face were both identified with personal being; thus a person's words as well as his face were means of confrontation.

As the word *dâbar*, which meant "word," was used in Old Testament times it could signify "thing" and "event" as well as an oral or written word. It was often used to designate something done as well as something spoken; realizing the fullness of the word, we can understand why, when it did refer to something spoken, it was so easily identifiable with the person who spoke.

Yahweh's word was held to be the power of Yahweh himself. So it was that he created the heavens and the earth just by speaking. "And God said, 'Let there by light'; and there was light" (cf. Genesis 1:3-31). By no other means than speaking could the Jews conceive of God making the firmament, dry land, stars and sun, living creatures, and man. We have already mentioned how our words make our worlds; it is one of the new realizations of our day. The depth and universality of that insight is hinted at in the biblical story of creation. The same imagery is found in Psalm 148, Verse 5, where the highest heavens are told to praise the Lord, "For he commanded and they were created."

The word by which God creates is also his purpose in creation. A word goes forth from a speaker; it is the way he expresses himself outside of himself. But since, in Judeo-Christian thought, the word of God is identified with God, his expression outside of himself must at the same time be his purpose existing outside of himself. Just as we are in our bodies and our thought is in our words, so God's purpose is in his words. Since God, for the Jews, increasingly became the Source of all reality, and since his words were his power, those words once uttered had no final destiny other than God himself; in returning to him, they could not return empty. The much-quoted passage from Isaiah 55:10-11 makes the point: "For as the rain and the snow come down from heaven, and return not thither but water the earth, making it bring forth and sprout, giving seed to the sower and bread to the eater, so shall my word be that goes forth from my mouth; it shall not return to me empty, but it shall accomplish that which I purpose, and prosper in the thing for which I sent it."

Wherever God's words are, their very presence is "return to him." They lead to him even when proceeding from him because he himself is present in them.

The Jews felt that God was at least akin to their being when they proclaimed that he created by speaking, but that kinship was not one which explained God to them. It was more a way of trying to see themselves in God's eyes than trying to see God in their eyes—that is, their conscious effort was to place themselves within God's primacy rather than to make God clear to human thought. As the verse preceding the ones we have quoted from Isaiah says, God's ways are higher than our ways, his thoughts higher than our thoughts. Because they are "spoken" by God, men cannot fully understand themselves or their world—let alone God himself. There is mystery in creation; in fact, creation is constituted by mystery: the mystery of God's speech which is mirrored in the mystery of man's speech.

St. Paul drew upon the might of the Word of God when he said in II Corinthians 4:6: "For it is the God who said, 'Let light shine out of darkness,' who has shown in our hearts to give the light of the knowledge of the glory of God in the face of Christ." Here we see again the connection between word and face. God's word is "seen" in the face of Jesus Christ. Because God's Word is creative and because we can live in Christ through the Spirit, Paul could rightly conclude that "if anyone is in Christ, he is a new creation" (II Corinthians 5:17).

In the same Epistle to the Corinthians, St. Paul goes on

to say: "Behold, now is the acceptable time; behold, now is the day of salvation" (6:2). St. Paul was speaking to a specific situation in the life of the Corinthians when he wrote his letter, but that need not keep us from seeing additional meaning in his words, based on the analysis contained in the last chapter. We noted there that the act of speaking always takes place in the present.

The Father speaks to us through his Word, the Son; wherever and whenever that Word exists, therefore, the Father is speaking to us. Since the message of Easter is that the incarnate Word always continues to exist, we must conclude that God is always speaking his creative Word to us in our present. Only *now* is the acceptable time to God, for, by definition, now is the time he is *speaking* to us. Now is the time we must listen to him. The Word by which we are sustained in God's creative might is neither a fading echo of the past nor an empty hope for the future.

Jesus Christ is God's final Word to man. As the Father's last word, there is nothing more the Father has to say to us; his self-expression (revelation) is complete. Still, the Word became flesh and, as flesh (man), is temporal, unfolding itself historically. We must say then that God's Word, although final in itself, is still working itself out in time, constantly revealing new modes of its consummate richness to us. In this sense, *now* is the acceptable time for us, because the future somehow informs it. For the Christian, God's last Word does not end a conversation; it initiates an ongoing dialogue which is one with the ongoing life of the universe. Can such a dialogue be escapement?

These considerations lead us immediately and naturally

to the trinitarian life of God. God the Father, Source of all being and all creation, Christians believe, reveals himself to man and gives himself to man. Because it is the Christian experience that God reveals and gives *himself*, the overwhelming conviction of that experience has been that God can be nothing less than a revealing and a giving in himself. Such a conviction about the nature of the divine life is symbolized in the doctrine of the Trinity. While remaining himself, the Father utters the Word which is his expression; such a Word, being the express image of the Father, is the only-begotten Son upon whom the Father bestows his love (the Spirit), his all-sufficient Gift. The God of Christians *is* knowledge and love—he does not just have them as activities that are less than he—because his very life is one of revealing and giving. We cannot understand the trinitarian life of God in conceptually clear terms. How could man hope to understand God? Still, understood for what it tries to do, the doctrine of the Trinity does more to explicate belief in a self-sufficient Source of reality that is living and personal than any alternative of which I am aware. It enables God in a properly mysterious way to be mutuality and thereby the all-sufficient Source for human life as our latest secular insights would describe that life.

The familiar prologue to St. John's Gospel begins: "In the beginning was the Word, and the Word was with God, and the Word was God. He was in the beginning with God; all things were made through him, and without him was not anything made that was made. . . . And the Word became flesh and dwelt among us, full of grace and truth; we have beheld his glory, glory as of the only Son from the Father" (1:1-3, 14). When Jesus was teaching in the temple, he said, "If you knew me, you would know my Father also" (John 8:19). Another time, when speaking to Philip, Jesus said: "He who has seen me has seen the Father" (John 14:9).

The Word is the Father *as the Father expresses himself.* The Word, it may be said, is the Father's exteriorization. God the Father is the Source and Sender of all; the Word is the Father as seen and sent. That means, as Karl Rahner has pointed out, that he who has seen the incarnate Word, Jesus Christ, has indeed seen the Father, for the Word which is incarnate is the Father precisely as seen (expressed).[1]

The Word is seen in Christ for what the Word is in himself, namely, the revelation of the Father. In Jesus Christ, "God as expression" comes to us expressed—as a man. As Rahner reiterates so frequently, to say that man is the "image of God" is to say that man is in a special way the expression of God. From evidence other than Christian sources, as examined in the last chapter, we have seen that it makes good sense to think of man as being himself a word. To learn from Christian sources that it is also as word (expression) that man resembles God is another instance of converging insights which make Christianity exciting today.

Before proceeding to the consequences for our lives of our relations to God through words, several illustrations of how Jesus was associated in New Testament times with the Word of God may be helpful.

[1] Karl Rahner, *Theological Investigations,* Vol. IV: *More Recent Writings,* trans. by Kevin Smyth (Baltimore: Helicon Press, 1966), p. 92 f.

A common designation of Jesus by his contemporaries was "rabbi," but although he was known by that common name, he was not thought by his disciples to be a common teacher. When Jesus explicated the Law, he stood much more as its judge than it stood as his judge. A feature of New Testament exegesis which pervades almost all schools of thought is the unique personal claim Jesus made for himself by such characteristic means of expression as "Verily, verily I say unto you . . ." or "But I say to you . . ." What Jesus said emanated so completely from his own being that his disciples found it impossible to separate him from his words. He was so much his words that he was finally accepted as the Word of God.

The word of God was for the Jews, we have seen, a powerful word. The connection between word and power is clearly seen in our Lord's conversation after the Last Supper, recounted in John 14:10 f.: "The words that I say to you I do not speak on my own authority; but the Father who dwells in me does his works. Believe me that I am in the Father and the Father in me; or else believe me for the sake of the works themselves." Here we see that Jesus' oneness with the Father is the source of his communication; we also see that the oneness is so singular that it is nothing less than the message of the communication.

Additional evidence that the acceptance of Jesus as the incarnate Word developed continuously from the Jewish experience of God is found in the prologue of St. John's Gospel. After stating that "the Word became flesh and dwelt among us," we read that "we have beheld his glory, glory as of the only Son from the Father" (1:14). Such dwelling of the Word in glory among men would recall to every pious Jew who heard it Yahweh's "tabernacling" with men and the glory of God that filled the tent of meeting in Moses' day (Exodus 40:34 ff.; Numbers 14:10). The glory of God which was seen in the face of Christ was the glory of his Word: God has expressed himself to men in a way which can be both seen and heard.

The human world is essentially a world of words. Man has been able to change the world because he is not held captive within it; he can recall the past and anticipate the future while he is in the present. Our culture, which includes everything from chemistry to poetry and from engineering to metaphysics, grows as we are capable of making more and more distinctions in the reality of which we are a part. Human communication is one of nuances, of delicate shades of meaning, that are possible only because we are able to separate ourselves from an immediate situation even while we are in it. Although the new car buyer is delighted with the latest model he drives away from his dealer's showroom, he knows, while he luxuriates in it, that bigger and better things in automobiles lie only a few years ahead. He is just using the present until he can get what the future holds for him.

The separation-in-the-midst-of-presence which is embodied in our speaking enables us to be concerned with the future and to be oriented toward the "more." It is only because man is a creature of words that he can have God for his end; it is because I have the ability to transcend myself in speech that I am able to know my own insufficiency and have at least an inkling of the self-sufficiency of God. How fit that we are led to God by his Word. Our goal is more than we are, and the Word, because it is God, is more than we are too.

Created in the image of God, we are living words of God and therefore capable of dialogue with the Son. "Communicate or perish" is the essence of our being, for a word that does not communicate is no word at all, but only a sound. As speaking creatures, we can answer God. For that reason, we can be called. Answering the call we hear, we are *elected* by God to be his adopted sons, whereby we receive our vocation to become co-creators of his world in a union of love which has been proved stronger than death.

A well-worn Christian adage has it that faith comes by hearing (cf. Romans 10:17). Christian faith is response to God's incarnate Word, Jesus Christ. But St. Paul asked how men are to believe in someone of whom they have never heard, and he went on to ask how they can hear without a preacher. Proclamation of the Good News to all the world is the vocation of every Christian. Incorporated by their baptism into the Word, being the Word's expression of the Father is their new life. Proclamation of the Word is the foundation of everything Christian. In a manner analogous to the way the word defines the human world, faith, the hearing of God's Word, defines the new world we receive from God. Only human beings can have faith because only they can *hear*. It was the word uttered by the great prophets of old that enabled the Israelites to see God's action in their history; it was such speaking and hearing that enabled the Jews' history to be a vehicle of faith. The word enabled Jewish history to be a salvation history.

Hosea's prophecy was rooted in the history of his
people. He chastized the Jews of his day by comparing
their relationship to God with the relationship of his own
unfaithful wife to him, but he illustrated a more obvious
love between God and his chosen people in their deliver-
ance from Egypt under the guidance of Moses, another
prophet with the word of God. Amos and Isaiah were
spokesmen for the divine law: Amos exposed and con-
demned the social injustice of his day; Isaiah did the
same, extending his proclamations to the troubled international scene as well. He especially saw individual acts
in the light of a wider context of saving history. The warnings of Jeremiah about Israel's impending doom were
commentaries on his nation's worship of foreign gods. He
saw the Babylonians as agents of God's wrath. Elijah and
Elisha in earlier times tried to keep the Lord's people
from worshiping the Baal. Through the *word*, the Israelites were led to see God's hand working everywhere, in
the events of nature and in the lives of nations.

In a related manner, words structure Christian history
and define the nature of the sacraments. The Word exists
outside the sacraments calling people to them, but the
Word is not merely preparatory and external to a properly
developed sacramental life. That Word also exists within
the sacraments, telling what they are and establishing the
context of faith in the community which alone enables the
sacraments to be themselves. The faith of the Christian
community is the location of the sacraments; Christ's
promise cannot be received outside that location. It is in
that sense that he taught as he healed, "Your faith has
made you well" (Mark 10:52).

To hear God's Word is to be transformed by the Word. "The words that I have spoken to you are spirit and life" (John 6:63). "If you continue in my word, you are truly my disciples, and you will know the truth, and the truth will make you free" (John 8:31). To keep Christ's word is to love him and to have the Father and the Son come to dwell with the hearer (cf. John 14:23 f.). Any truly Christian word, even though only spoken, has power to change a person, for as a Christian word it is God's expression of himself; it is God influencing our lives through personal dialogue with us. Since God is personal power and the Word is God, truly to hear the Word enables God to be present with power to the hearer. To hear God's Word is an event in one's life, the event of being with God.

God can be personally present with a hearer through spoken or written words alone, but because of the limitations of such words and the infinite richness of God, hearing and reading are not sufficient means of the Word's presence. God's Word is too efficacious to be limited to sounds in the air and ink marks on paper when calling our attention to the Father's love. The creativity of the Word is so great that its presence demands expression beyond the channels of audible speaking and two-dimensional printing. In the sacrament of the Holy Communion, above all other sacraments, the Word is conveyed with a fullness that obviously exceeds the mode of oral-aural communication.

In the Eucharist, God calls his people together by means of heralds commissioned through baptism and ordination; the people respond to the call of Christ throughout the world by assembling to hear the proclamation of God's Word in the Holy Scripture and in preaching. The implications of such an assembly are so basic and far-reaching that it will be worth our while to pause here a moment to consider them. We must see the full force of the fact that God always *calls* his people. We can be helped in so doing if we consider what is involved in the calling we do in our ordinary lives; Christianity helps us in our everyday lives, and those lives can, in turn, help us understand Christianity.

We have all called someone. How did we do it?

By using words.

"Billy come here!" we say. After waiting a moment we may have to add, "Please put that paper down and come immediately!" When a father calls his son in that manner, he is trying to enter his son's life in a new way. Whenever we call someone, we interrupt him. Billy's life was going on the way he wished it to, sitting in the living room reading the paper instead of joining the family at the dinner table. It was in order to interrupt Billy's previously set pattern of living that his father called him.

If Billy is polite and answers his father, his answer consists in turning from what he has been doing and asking his father what he wants. In the fullest response he can give to his father's call, Billy does not just sit where he is and shout back; he gets up and goes to his father in order to ask what he wants. He becomes, in other words, *available* to his father. Putting the paper down, getting up, and going to the person who called him is actually the most complete answer Billy can give to that person's call, for by his physical presence he most completely makes himself available to the caller. Generalizing from Billy's action, we can see that whenever we answer someone, that person becomes the primary consideration in our lives at that moment. In fact, another person becomes primary in our lives only to the extent that we answer him; that is what answering *him* means. By responding to a call, we open ourselves to something new and different.

Answering someone's call is a way we can become more than we were. An invitation, no matter how formally it may be printed, is actually a call from some one to us. Many of our earliest invitations were literally made by the vocal calls of our friends to us, and some of the best invitations we receive in adult life are made the same way. It is the way spontaneous parties start. Whenever we answer an invitation or a call, we leave our old selves, thereby making ourselves available for something new. Being with others, we become more than we would have been if we stayed home alone.

Christianity is, above all, the call of God to us. Such a call is the nature of the whole Christian religion, because the Son is the Word of the Father sent to us. That Word comes to break into our lives so that it can bring something new to us. God sends his Word into the world so that we will turn toward him and answer him. Our turning toward him is called conversion; our answer to him is called faith.

The Christian Word, because it is a *call*, is something special; it is a demand. It is a Word that makes a difference. When it is recognized for what it is, it is a happening; where *it* is heard, it is an event that involves our whole lives. That is why it cannot be reduced to ink on the pages of a Bible or sounds heard in a church building.

If we hear it for what it is—a call—it will move us to do something. What? To proclaim it and give thanks for it. To hear God's Word is to have a personal encounter with God. Such an encounter is always a living experience in the present; thus, wherever God's Word is itself, it compels our ongoing proclamation of it in the present. The Word of God cannot be read or heard as if it were past, abstract, finished, or something to be used by us. It uses us. By rejoicing in it, we give ourselves so completely to it that we in one sense become it; to the extent that we become it, we are its proclamation.

Realizing that the Word is God's call to us, the presence of the Word in the Holy Eucharist enables the recent emphasis on congregational standing during the Eucharist to be understood. (Standing is the ancient posture for the divine liturgy and is now being revived in the liturgical revisions of several Western churches.) The Holy Eucharist itself can be considered a call to us; Christians, therefore, stand during it to show, in the most obvious way possible, that they are there to answer God and make themselves available to him. Rejoicing in the fact that God has noticed them by his call, it is only fitting that they should place their full selves at his disposal. "Eucharist" means "thanksgiving"; can a person give thanks while sitting or kneeling? He can to some extent, but if his feeling of gratitude is as total as possible, does it not force him to his feet? We kneel in supplication, but we jump to our feet in joy. We do not want to be held back from a person to whom we are grateful; we naturally get up and go to him to express our thanks. Crowds spontaneously jump to their feet to express their thanksgiving at football games;

perhaps it is the lack of that much joy and thanksgiving which has kept them off their feet in their worship of God.

Standing at God's disposal during the Holy Eucharist and, indeed, figuratively throughout our whole lives, we will find it more difficult to put Jesus into the pigeonholes we have for him. The way many people kneel and sit in church, they are very obviously withdrawing into themselves; they sit or kneel with a slouch and become less attentive rather than more attentive to what they are doing when they pray. To meet Jesus in that manner is to tell him before we utter a word that we will only meet him on our terms. His people, his world, his primacy, are not our first concern. By such a simple action as standing for at least some of our most profound worship, we make it harder for ourselves to clamp God into our preconceived categories and to accept him only according to our prefelt needs.

Since we assemble for the Holy Eucharist only because of God's call, while we are so assembled, it must be for his purpose. That purpose is the thanksgiving of his Son in the Spirit of the Son. To let our motives interfere with Jesus' primacy by being concerned with him only to the extent that he answers *our* requests, or to disguise his act of thanksgiving by our private devotions of a different tone, is to refuse his invitation in his presence. It is to answer his call in order to ignore him.

The primary element in Christianity is God's call to us, the sending of his Word to us in order to help us become more than we are. The proclamation and hearing of the Word in the Holy Eucharist are not abstract activities, segregated from our lives in the world. As we have indicated, the Word of God always has the fullness of a concrete historical event. As such, the proclamation and hearing of God's Word based on the Holy Scripture are actually historical prolongations of the very actions we read about in the Old and New Testaments. To hear God's Word is to be taken up into the continuous and never-ending movement of the Word in history. To hear God's Word in the Old Testament prophets, for example, is to be engaged in prophetic activity in the present; it is not to hear stories about quaint religious critics of the past.

Having considered some of the general implications of the nature of God's Word as a call, we may now return to our consideration of the modes of the Word's expression in the Holy Eucharist. We have already pointed out that God's people are called together by his heralds to hear his Word read and proclaimed. Written and spoken words, however, even in the sense in which they are events of encounter with God, are not adequate to the Good News we have in Christ. Christ is truly present in the Word verbally proclaimed, but he wills to be present through other modes of location also. Love cannot express itself by words alone, even though they be Spirit-filled. Therefore, in the Eucharist, the Word comes to us through more than words when the bread and wine become the mystical body and blood of Christ through their incorporation by the Word into the pattern of the Word's incarnate life.

In dialogue with us through the society he forms by his free choice (the Church) and which is perfected by the consummating action of his Son (the Eucharist), God constitutes us so that we can give his meaning to the world in our continuing dialogue with it. That meaning is the Word. Insofar as the body is the existence type of the world, we have seen that the body determines the nature of the world; in addition, the activities we carry on through our words define the world. In a similar way, the Church as the body of Christ, and thus as the Word of God in the world, determines the nature of God's redeemed world.

Through the consecration of the material elements of bread and wine in the Eucharist, God's Word continually breaks into his assembled community in an embodied, concrete way, to keep that community open to himself and to the universe. Because the consecrating activity of the Eucharist always involves new members of the physical world through the repeated use of bread and wine and newly expressed acts of cooperation on the part of God's people, God's calling Word is meant to keep the Christian community from becoming introverted and sedimented in the past. The eucharistic presence of God's Word is his constant act of saying something new to us in the present. In the eucharistic Christ the Word is intimately present with God's people through a physical location, something that is especially appropriate to people who are themselves physically located words.

The presence of the Word with man in the sacramental body of Christ is meant to keep men available to the "other"—to God, to other men, and to the universe. The nature of "word" is "availability to others." In the Eucharist we are given food to embrace the new, the unfamiliar, the threatening. As fed by Christ's body we are led by the Word into a life of active synthesis in the dialogue he carries on with us through his creation; we are called to a life of growing meaning and confrontation, one that is meant to progress from "glory to glory."

Insofar as we are Christians, we should see all speech centering in the Holy Communion where the Word speaks from his fullest presence. Man's first word, we have seen, can be called a body-word, an often ambiguous type of expression which needs the perfection of the spoken word to become its true self. Our bodies are constituted by our words: our bodies are not just *things*, because our words in one sense arise from them and expand our location in the world which is first due to them. Jesus Christ as the incarnate Word is the Body-Word which is our goal rather than an ambiguous beginning which must be perfected. We know that our speech must always be from one point of view rather than another. In Jesus Christ, God the Father tells us that being a "point of view" is an essential feature of the human condition, and he goes on to be the point of view which is his saving expression in human life.

We live in the midst of many different language systems. In addition to the languages of the sciences, there is the language of the suburbs and the language of the cities' inner core; there are the languages of different ethnic groupings of men, and there are the languages of different generations. School children in a family frequently speak quite a different language from their parents and their grandparents. Different cultures and subcultures express things in different ways; Orientals such as the Chinese express reverence by making noise and shooting off firecrackers, whereas Westerners usually show reverence by

silence. "Cool" means to remain detached and uninvolved
in one language system of the youth of today, while in
another it indicates involvement and participation. To set
a business appointment at 5 P.M. in a Latin country means
something quite different from what it means in the
United States. In the United States the appointment
would probably be the last one for the day, and quickly
coming to the point and getting the business over with
would be a requirement understood by everybody
present; in Latin countries, on the other hand, people
would be offended if one tried to talk business with them
as soon as he arrived. Misunderstandings that arise because of our use of different language systems have now
become so obvious that an International Society for Overcoming the Language Barrier has been established.

Because in authentic speaking man is his language and
because we must always be "points of view" in our personal lives, the quest for a universal human language
seems doomed to failure. We have only to look at the
language difficulties caused by the generation gap between parents and children in our families to be convinced that many languages can exist within one tongue.
If men remain truly persons, there can be no shortcut to
understanding each other by means of a formally unified
language. Men become unified by understanding more
about each other as they already exist rather than by trying to reduce one another to a common denominator by
formal agreements. Men may one day agree on a common
tongue, but they will never be able to live with only one
language. The presence of the Word in the Eucharist—
the re-calling of the Word-become-man—is the paradigm

for our speaking to other men in the language they understand. It is the central source of grace for our communication as persons with other persons; it is meant to be the source from which our words are humanized by God.

In the eucharistic presence the Word comes to man as man. God's Word calls men to him for what they are rather than reducing them to what they are not. God's Word is a creative, enriching Word, one that can guide us through history because it unfolds itself in history. It is a Word which leads us into intensified personal relationships because it is the Word who is Person, not a word which categorizes others for the sake of mechanical convenience. We mechanically dismiss people by our words, however, whenever we categorize them as no more than "black," "white," "rich," "poor," "teen-ager," "adolescent," "senile," "paranoic," "schizophrenic," "show-off," "dunce," "hood," "hypochondriac."

By becoming man, the Word has shown us how we are to become men. We are to speak to others where they are for what they are; we are to be God's words with them rather than merely "having words" with them. As we participate in the eucharistic activity, receiving the Word with the same historical precision with which the Son lived on earth, we become more completely God's expression. We become, through grace, special words who can reveal God's love through either silence or sound. Eating his Word, we won't have to eat ours.

The different language systems available to us constitute a primary area in which our freedom is exercised. We have a choice of describing a flower in the language of physics, chemistry, botany, commerce, history, art, geometry, metaphysics, or poetry. In the Holy Eucharist we celebrate that freedom in God's own terms, giving thanks to him through our words for his Word, and being consecrated by his Word to express the freedom of his love in the world. The Church consecrates physical elements from the world (and, by intention, the whole world in those elements) by its words and actions of thanksgiving; God, in turn, consecrates his people and their world by the action of his Word upon them. Receiving God's Word with the historical fullness of the ongoing activity of his Church, the body of Christ, partakers of the Holy Communion should find it impossible to use their words against their fellowmen and equally impossible not to want to know what their fellowmen are saying to them. The Eucharist supplies modern man with motivation for dialogue with his fellows, by allowing him no alternative to it: the Eucharist makes motivation to dialogue coextensive with man's being because in the Eucharist man's being is totally defined by the Word. Participating in the dialogue of God's own being through God's Word, we show our conviction that there is no final alternative to dialogue anywhere in being.

Young people such as the "hippies" of our day are disgusted with hearing empty words. But if hippies have been keen in their insight into the verbal hypocrisy of the older generation, the keenness of their analysis has been hidden from many of the people whose hypocrisy they have exposed—because of the hippies' often passive reaction to their own discoveries. The older generation gets the message of protest much less equivocally from members of the Peace Corps, for example, who are overtly trying to do what others have left undone.

Christ is the Word who is action; in him word and creation cannot be separated. To have one's life centered in the Eucharist, then, is to have one's life centered in an ongoing activity which, because it is so complete, must be proclaimed. Because the proclamation is grounded in activity, the very activity of God in Christ, the proclamation without the activity is not the proclamation at all. Marshall McLuhan's slogan that "the medium is the message" has got to be true of the incarnate Word! Here as nowhere else the medium of proclamation is the message proclaimed. We have seen that human words always require separation from what they refer to; they always point beyond themselves. They can be used for deceit as well as for revelation. With that in mind, it can be said that we must be religious "beneath the level of words": we must be religious at a level of commitment that is more basic than a conventional use of language. We must be our words.

Under such circumstances it would be impossible not to follow the advice given in the Epistle of St. James: "But be doers of the word, and not hearers only, deceiving yourselves" (1:22). The First Epistle of St. John correctly states our relationship to the Word in saying: "Little children, let us not love in word or speech but in deed and in truth" (3:18).

Our intimacy with the Word by cooperating in his thanksgiving to the Father continued among us in the Eucharist gives God's wholeness to our lives. Erwin Straus has remarked that sound homogenizes space. Space is differentiation, for each "part" of it is outside of every other part. If a person's life is confused, we naturally describe it in spatial metaphors by saying that it is cluttered up, upside down, or compartmentalized. We speak of people "spreading themselves too thin." Sound, however, unifies; it permeates space with a oneness that is foreign to space. So the Word of God homogenizes the different activities of our lives, our life-space, by giving us the same thing to do everywhere. Saying but one thing to us, "Jesus Christ," it is present with us everywhere: it surrounds us as sound does in a room; it directs us as a call does in a crowd; it demands our response as a question does in a conversation.

We express ourselves in words because we are ourselves only in our bodies. Christ's body is the Word incarnate, and we are Christians only to the extent that we believe in the resurrection of the body as we have earlier described that resurrection. The everlasting existence of Christ's body is the most convincing way the Father could tell embodied persons such as we of the unending significance of Christ's mission. The resurrected body is the only body of Christ which now exists; that is the body we receive in a sacramental mode in the Holy Communion. Every time we receive the Lord's body, we are being told by that fact that our words are important and that they are meant to be informed by the Word. What could be a more significant message for God's last word to us?

VI ✤ "Let's Get Together
Sometime"

How common is the remark "Let's get together sometime," and how often it is made when we do not know
what else to say during a conversation with a friend. Most
frequently, the getting together never takes place, for neither the place nor the time for a meeting has been set. No
real invitation has been given. Once again we note that
general wishes are insufficient to make any real change in
our lives.

Still, human beings need to get together. Our need at
this point in history is evidently greater than our desire.
We have had two major wars in this century plus a number of smaller ones. There is armed conflict in the world at
the moment of this writing, and threats of additional conflicts are felt on more than one continent.

Even within nations we are not living very well together. Every nation in the world has some internal problems. Russia, for example, has embarked on another anti-
Semitic campaign. And recently, within one week's time,
there were civil disturbances in thirty-one cities in twelve

states in the United States; the patterns of such disruptions have not always been the same in southern and northern cities, but we know that things have not been right in Watts, Newark, Detroit, Selma, New York, Minneapolis, Jackson, Milwaukee, Phoenix, and Mobile. Whether the particular spark that ignites a disturbance be called racial, economic, educational, personal, or political, it is necessarily *social*. We are not living well together.

Where the greatest numbers of our people are congregated, we frequently find the greatest degree of isolation. There are many ways we get away from each other, and most of them have been clearly exposed by present-day prophets and analysts. We change our neighborhood; we move to the suburbs; we segregate others in various geographical, social, political, economic, and educational pockets; we immerse ourselves in escapist entertainment; we spin on cocktail rounds; we inhale, swallow, or inject psychedelic drugs.

It has been the contention of this book that the eucharistic pattern of Christian living takes us as we are in order to make us and our world what we are not—God-like. Now it is time for us to focus our attention on man's social nature. As we mentioned in the Introduction, that nature is not always obvious today. The statement that man is a social animal is not a new one, but the evidence gathered from our society sometimes makes us wonder how it could be an old one. As we have also previously remarked, society seems to be the very thing producing antisocial behavior and impersonal relations. It is sometimes difficult to find, in a given person's life, healthy roots from which the communal dimension of the Christian life can grow. Let us now examine the interpersonal constitution of our being with a consideration of material we have not yet discussed and a refocusing of some previous material. A leading figure in the field of psychoanalysis and developmental psychology, Erik H. Erikson of Harvard University, states that clinical practice has led him to recognize in every human being a threefold process of organization: organic, ego, and societal.[1] As a physical organism, a person's being is a process of integration aiming at homeostasis; the ego, in Erikson's terminology, is the organizing principle of a person's total experience aiming at "ego identity" and continuity through change; the social principle of integration tries to organize interpersonal relations into an affirmative whole. A neurosis can be described from any one of the three points of view; but, in order to be fully understood, Erikson contends, it must be described from all three.

Evidence indicates that there is no one cause of an anxiety or a neurosis. Each of the three aspects of man which have been listed contributes to a neurosis by influencing the intolerances of the other two aspects. A physical deficiency (exhaustion, a lesion, fever, palpitation, pain) influences a person's ego and social tolerances, while an ego upset (such as an unexpected challenge to a basic belief) affects both a person's physical and social relations. The pervasiveness of social factors in man's life is in many ways the most recent area of discovery. Professor Erikson, as we have indicated, believes that every anxiety has a communal aspect; for example, a young child's psycho-

[1] Erik H. Erikson, *Childhood and Society*, second edition (New York: W. W. Norton & Co., 1963), p. 36.

logical difficulties always correspond to a neurotic problem of his mother;[2] "there is no individual anxiety which does not reflect a latent concern common to the immediate and extended group."[3] Dr. J. H. van den Berg has been so impressed with the effects of community membership and group exclusion in an individual's life that he has suggested the word "sociosis" be substituted for "neurosis."[4]

Dr. van den Berg, like Professor Erikson, stresses the fundamental nature of membership in a group, of life in a world-with-others, for full personal development. Everything essentially human is found in some world we occupy with other people. Sex may be taken as an example; it is obviously a way of living with others. A more specific example from within the general area of sex will serve to illustrate Dr. van den Berg's basic contention: he instances the fainting of a Victorian woman at the advances of her lover in either marriage or courtship. Girls of the Victorian era were isolated from the human world of sex in their upbringing. The reproduction of plants and animals may have been taught to them; but human sex was not discussed in their presence, and even their clothing hid their sexuality rather than acknowledging it. Having been raised in a humanly asexual world for years—because it "preserved" them for their future husbands—when, suddenly, they were forced by society into the world of courtship and marriage, that new world was to-

[2] *Ibid.*, p. 30.
[3] *Ibid.*, p. 36.
[4] J. H. van den Berg, *The Changing Nature of Man: Introduction to a Historical Psychology*, trans. by H. F. Croes (New York: Delta Books, 1964), Ch. 3.

tally strange to them. They were not prepared to live in it; they did not understand how human communication took place within it. Not knowing how to respond to its demands and how to act with others in such a world, all they could do was try to leave it as quickly as possible. Fainting was the surest exit! Psychologically, fainting means that a person has "no group to belong to"; it is a way of avoiding a strange world and of testifying to one's lack of personal resources in it. The psychological factors which provoke fainting or any other neurotic behavior pattern always have a sociological or communicative structure, according to Dr. van den Berg; hence, the appropriateness of his term "sociosis."

The most immediate group involved in a person's life, of course, is the family. Very often a neurosis or psychosis is only a manifestation in one individual of a whole family's crisis.[5] But group crisis or group panic can also spread to a nation. The ethnic identity of the Jewish people and the persecutions they have suffered throughout their history have proved especially critical in their individual lives. What can keep group identification and group panic from spreading to the whole world?

Erikson believes that there can be no ego development outside of society, for only in society can be found on display the persons and roles upon which personal growth can be patterned. Trust, the earliest experience of mutuality, is first learned from an infant's relation with its

[5] C. F. Midelfort has continued to develop this insight since his book *The Family in Psychotherapy* (New York: McGraw-Hill Book Co., Inc.) appeared in 1957. He has found great benefit in family-centered therapy and even uses members of a client's family as hospital attendants if the hospitalization of a patient is necessary.

mother. Doubt and shame, as well as encouragement and
support, are first experienced in the family. Initiative and
guilt, industry and inferiority, identity and intimacy—all
involve relations with others.[6]

Man's whole development can thus be described in
interpersonal terms. That is well and good and would
be enough descriptively to show that man can be himself
only with others. A bit later we will turn to other psychologists and psychoanalysts for additional information
about man's social nature; before we do, however, themes
that we have already partially developed such as "body,"
"word," and "world" can furnish us with even deeper reasons why man must in some sense *be* community. Dealing
with man's body, his expression as word, and his world,
we are dealing with the most basic elements of his constitution; no more ultimate reasons for his social nature can
be found.

We are social in the sense that relationship to others
permeates every aspect of our being. We will examine
that permeation now in relation to the topics we have just
mentioned: world, body, and word.

It cannot be denied that everything we are, we are in
the world, and everything we do, we do in the world;
there simply are no other alternatives. But the world in
which we live is not a container into which we are thrown
like tacks in a box. That would be to think of man as a
thing within another *thing*. Man makes his world by being
in it; he does not find it ready-made.[7] Georges Gusdorf's

[6] Cf. Erikson, *Childhood and Society*, Ch. 7.
[7] Cf. Arthur A. Vogel, *The Next Christian Epoch* (New York: Harper
and Row, 1966), Chs. 1, 5.

remark that man lives not in a natural milieu but in a historical, cultural one is right to the point.[8] Persons and our relations to persons are prior to things. The kinds of bodies we are and the kind of words we use help constitute the kind of world in which we live.

The world of each one of us is a field of meaning centered in our lived experience; that experience and that meaning are essentially related to others. It has been well said that we exist *through* others, not just with them. We are not related to each other like marbles in a bag. Being persons with conscious interiority and depth, we are constituted in the core of our being by our relationships with one another. That is the basis of the mutuality we have already discussed, and it will be the basis of the reciprocity among persons we are going to discuss. Attitudes, words, and behavior define our world, and all of these depend on relations with others.

A sense of community will overwhelm us to the degree we realize that our body locates us in reality. The difficulty is that too many of us try to know ourselves by introspection alone; to try to make exclusive use of such knowledge denies the kind of being we are. As we have noted innumerable times, we are our bodies. The attempt to deny that fact by thinking we can know about ourselves through introspection alone perverts our whole relation to the world. We then try to view the world as nothing more than a spectacle or a show passing before us which we are free to look at or not as we wish. Actually, as we have tried to show, we can do no such thing; we *are*

[8] Georges Gusdorf, *Mythe et métaphysique: Introduction à la philosophie* (Paris: Flammarion, 1953), p. 277.

relation-to-the-world because we are embodied persons. We are not pure centers of consciousness with no location in the world, and we are not free arbitrarily to look at the world from any point of view we wish.

Because we are our bodies, we not only have an outside but we are our outside. *We* are seen by others; they do not see just a shadow of us or a machine that we are driving. They see us. Thus it is from others as well as from ourselves that we must learn what we are. We lack, in our interior knowledge of ourselves, the aspects of us others see. To be a man is to be seen. Our bodies make us social. The Greeks thought the body individuated man and was the principle of his separateness, and to a certain extent they were right; but when the meaning of the body is fully developed, it also turns out to be the principle of man's communal nature. Incarnation is our bond with other persons; to realize that I am seen by others is to realize my community with them.

The sensual perception we have of each other because of our bodies condemns us to live in the same world, even though some of us may not like the fact. Unsocial behavior is itself expressed through the body, necessarily revealing itself to others. Is not the most aberrant and individualistic behavior meaningful only in the presence of the community it wishes to deny?

Located by others through the perception of our bodies, we must recognize that our lives and thoughts have historical limitations. The man who refuses to recognize his limitations is not by that fact unlimited; he is the more severely limited because of his ignorance. Because of our bodies, we cannot help but live in a certain time and place and be at least partially defined by our relations to others. The possibilities of even the most revolutionary thinkers are largely determined by the culture in which they live. Einstein could not have been himself in ancient Greece, nor Beethoven in primitive Africa. The subculture of the hippies in our day requires our day. If they were not produced by our culture, they could not protest it; that they were produced by it gives what significance there is to their protest.

Continuing with the ramifications of our embodiment, we should recall that our perception itself involves inter-subjectivity. As soon as I recognize that my perception occurs from a certain point of view, I have tacitly acknowledged that another person can perceive the same thing that I do from a different point of view.

The way we see and hear things depends upon the world-field in which we perceive them. A primitive tribesman from Australia would not perceive the same things in New York City that a native of that city perceives. Looking at the same color patches and listening to the same sounds, he would see and hear different things, for all perception takes place within a field of meaning that both extends beyond and qualifies every individual perception we have.

The nature of human perception we are now describing contrasts significantly to the nature of mechanical perception as the latter has so far been developed. The photo-electric cells used in what are presently called "perceptrons" (learning machines that can adapt themselves to conditions not programmed into them ahead of time) are passive reporters of every optical pattern of light and shade which can trigger them—that is to say, such machines report with equal emphasis every optical pattern they are capable of recognizing. Their operation is analogous to the way a tape recorder picks up every noise in a room. Because human perception, on the other hand, is always in a world—in a specific context—it does not indiscriminately recognize everything that goes on. It sees only what it is looking for and hears only what it is listening for. Instead of hearing every noise in a crowded room, a man is able to hear only the voice of his wife; after a while people who live near railway tracks no longer hear the trains.

There is a selective activity in animal perception that has not yet been matched in cybernation. The "ground" within which we see a "figure" gives meaning to the figure. In that way we ourselves are active contributors to the meaning of events in our world. Things are at least partially defined by their relations to the meaning-field within which they stand, and it is our selectivity which enables them to stand as figures in such a field. A hunter looks only for animal movement in the bushes; a detective looks for clues; a mineralogist sees iron ore in a stone; a mother listens to her child playing in a band. Perception requires that something be in the foreground; what is there and what can come there depends, in turn, upon the world-view of the perceiver.

Something social is found in every sensation we have, for our sensations are meaningful to us, and human meaning is always communal. We see what our interpersonal relations enable us to see. The focus of our attention is person-directed by means of the cultural milieu in which we live.

Of all the animals known, man is the least controlled by heredity and instinct. That is to say, man is the animal most conditioned by society. The most extreme differences among men are cultural differences, for, abstractly considered, all human beings have remarkably similar capabilities and potentialities. That men who start out with similar potentialities end up actually so different is primarily explained by the different societies in which they mature. A boy of pure Chinese stock who is raised by Americans finds it just as difficult to adjust to the Chinese manner of life as an American boy raised by Americans does.

We have seen that the role words play in our thinking is due to our incarnation; but words are themselves only in a language, and a language, as Saussure reminded us, is always communal. No man possesses a language, although he can possess a considerable vocabulary within a language. We need words that already mean something if we are going to be able to express ourselves through them. We have to assimilate a vocabulary before we can express ourselves in a foreign language, and we go through the same kind of process in learning our native tongue. Here we find an illustration of how freedom should be related to community. Having something done by others before we act, having something in hand to work with, enables us to be free. Having freedom of choice in our use of words depends first upon our having words of established meaning to choose from. The indispensable service of community to individual persons is to locate them for freedom. A community perverts its role and becomes oppressive, on the other hand, when it over-locates a person, externally positioning him and thus denying him the freedom, future, and choice that constitute his nature as a person.

Words and the communal experience they embody are a primary means by which relationship to others qualifies our most intimate lives. We are best able to perceive what we can identify, and the process of identification is again a group process. Education is the way distinctions that have significance within a community are communicated to new members of the community. Music appreciation, by teaching children the names of the instruments in an orchestra, enables them to hear the instruments in a new way. We see the colors we can name, as we also see the birds, trees, planets, and automobiles we know. A trained observer sees more than an untrained one, which is the reason for taking our cars to mechanics and ourselves to doctors.

The community formed by our bodies, words, and worlds is community we cannot help but be. Even it, however, needs community to be pointed out. All meaning is mutuality, a way of being together.

We spoke in the first chapter about the primacy of reality in healthy living and in healthy religion. Most psychological therapies, at least by intention, are attempts to let people accept reality. Nowhere is that contention more obviously stated than in Reality Therapy as developed by Dr. William Glasser.[9] Of special interest to us at the moment is the way Dr. Glasser understands human reality; his view speaks directly to the communal nature of man.

Dr. Glasser maintains that every human being has basic psychological needs which must be fulfilled if he is to be

[9] Cf. William Glasser, *Reality Therapy* (New York: Harper and Row, 1965).

himself: he needs to love and be loved, and he needs to feel worthwhile to himself and to others. People who are unable to fulfill their needs compensate for that fact by a denial of reality, and that denial, in turn, necessitates their behaving in irresponsible ways.

A person can learn to accept his real self only if *others* refuse to accept anything but his real self in their relations with him. That means, first of all, of course, that other people must have truly personal relations with him; Reality Therapy demands genuine involvement with the person who needs help. In the midst of such involvement, irresponsible behavior must be rejected, for only by the (loving) rejection of irresponsibility can the need for better ways of fulfilling one's basic needs be taught.

If we love another person for what he really is, we must respect his needs; but to respect his needs is to expect him to try to fulfill them. We show true love for another by expecting responsible behavior from him and not accepting anything less. The responsibility of a loving parent, Dr. Glasser states, is not to desert his child by expecting nothing from him; a teen-ager's nagging insistence that there be no restrictions upon him is frequently a disguised test to discover just how much his parents love him. Is their own comfort more important to them than he is? If so, he knows they will let him do anything in the end, as long as they can go on living their lives without interference.

The structure of human reality is the important thing; that is why therapy, in Dr. Glasser's view, should not be directed toward making a person happy. Being in the world with others is the condition of being happy, not vice versa. Happiness, it is found, most frequently occurs

where people are responsible in their behavior; certainly
that kind of happiness has the best chance of lasting.

As we actually exist, our world is first a world of action,
of behavior, a world of commitment and involvement. We
enter the world by acting in it; action is the mark of our
reality even if it is no more than an infant's crying, kicking, gurgling, eating, and sleeping. We are real because
we act, and our whole development as persons is affected
by the way other persons act toward us. That is why Reality Therapy stresses behavior rather than attitude. What
one does is more important than how one feels; behavior
changes attitudes more effectively than attitudes change
behavior. We become our full selves through interpersonal relations rather than through private feelings. We
begin our lives by "behaving," and we can be ourselves
only as long as we continue to behave!

The primacy of being with others and the basic role of
love in our lives are themes generally stressed in current
psychological literature. Among such books that have had
wide influence at the popular level is Erich Fromm's *The
Art of Loving*.[10] Dr. Fromm maintains that every human
being has a need for unity; attempts to achieve it may
take such forms as the orgiastic use of sex and alcohol,
sameness in group life, creative activity, and love. Love is
the most inclusive and satisfactory means of overcoming
isolation. In Dr. Fromm's eyes it is an art, something to be
practiced and something with rules that aid its practice.
Love is an activity, one which we alone are responsible
for and one which demands of us intensified and wakeful
vitality. It is not something we should passively expect to
receive from others; it is the means of our most productive

[10] New York: Bantam Books, 1963.

self-expression, not a prize we must wait to receive from others.

In his discussion of love, Dr. Fromm also stresses its universal and reciprocal nature. Brotherly love is that found among equals, and because the equals who are so loved have a common need, to love one of them is to love all of them. Erotic love is also among equals, but it differs from brotherly love because a *fusion* takes place between the loving parties. Because of that fusion, erotic love tends to be exclusive; people who have such a bond between them may, in the name of love, actually be selfish together. A man and woman "so much in love with each other" that they try to shut other people out of their lives are actually perverting love in love's own name. To love one person is to love all people. Since love is an activity, and in that sense a productive expression of one's power as a person, if someone is loving, his positive attitude will show everywhere toward all men. It will even show in his relation to himself. A loving person must love himself; in other words, he must be productive, in the deepest sense of the term, toward himself as well as toward others. True self-love is just the opposite of selfishness. Selfishness is narcissistic; it is emptiness and frustration which result from an unproductive withdrawal from the world.

Because personal productiveness should be itself in every situation in which it is found, Fromm concludes that properly to love one person is to love all persons. Love leads immediately to the communal nature of man. Similar conclusions have been reached from a different type of analysis by Maurice Nédoncelle.[11]

[11] Cf. Maurice Nédoncelle, *Love and the Person,* trans. by Sr. Ruth Adelaide (New York: Sheed and Ward, 1966).

Centers of consciousness have a necessary reciprocity, according to Nédoncelle; that reciprocity shows itself in varying degrees in the relationship of love. At its lowest degree, there is reciprocity between a lover and his beloved at least to the extent that the beloved gives himself to the world and allows himself to be seen in it. Such exposure is not a specific gift of himself to the lover, but any participation in the world involves some kind of self-commitment. That commitment has the general nature of love. We all too quickly learn the tactics of hypocrisy and defensive withdrawal within the world we share together, but love always looks in a person for the trust and commitment natural to a child.

A second stage of personal reciprocity is found when a person becomes consciously aware of another's loving intention toward him, even though he may reject it after recognizing it. In that case, the lover has at least played a part in his beloved's life and the two people have responded to each other. A third level of reciprocity occurs when the person loved responds positively instead of negatively to the loving intention offered him. At that level the person loved cooperates with the intention of the lover and makes his own positive contribution to it. He contributes variations to the theme proposed to him and thus becomes more himself through that theme. At the fourth and highest level, complete reciprocity is found. Here the person loved wills the advancement of the lover just as intently as the lover first wills his.[12]

In its essence, love wills the infinite perfection of the person who is loved and of the person who loves. Love is

[12] *Ibid.*, pp. 19-22.

not a self-subsisting activity, and so, of course, we do less than justice to it when we speak of it as we have just done, as if it were a living subject. Nédoncelle's point is that, in loving, every person also wants to be loved. That desire is not a selfish intrusion upon the outgoing nature of love, however, for a person who loves desires to be loved *only in his loving*. A lover wants to be loved as a lover, which means that he must be loving before he can be loved. In a sense, the desire to be loved is secondary and dependent upon a prior relationship to others, just as our knowledge of ourselves is secondary and dependent upon others. Because every person who loves is a center of consciousness, he cannot help knowing himself as well as others; knowing himself *in* his outgoing activity of love, he cannot help but recognize in himself the necessity of that love being acknowledged for what it is by another person. In that way, love can be satisfied with nothing less than full reciprocity and a community of persons within which such reciprocity is increasingly expressed.

Selfish exclusion is the opposite of love. Here the analyses of Nédoncelle and Fromm fall into step. Insofar as it is itself, love extends equally to all men and founds a community that includes all men. What is willed in love for one is willed for all, for all men are built up as persons by the one activity which is love.

Different steps are taken by love as we are related to people in different ways. But whether it be in the world of law, economics, or politics, the freedom and status we will for one person we will for all persons—if we love the one person for himself. Love is a total activity which ultimately aims at nothing less than totality. Incompleteness and fragmentation are foreign to it; that is why it can be the ultimate value Christians claim it to be. Love, being itself, makes others be themselves.

All the evidence we have examined in this book indicates that in community we are prepared for community; through human situations we are prepared to be human; through communication we are prepared for communication. Mutuality and reciprocity are the human condition. Our bodies cannot be left out of consideration because our first contact with another person—mother—is bodily. The most touching human experiences derive their meaning from touching: a child at its mother's breast, lovers in each other's arms, an injured person being ministered to by another. An abandoned child reaching for food and affection which are not there and the unnaturalness of isolation draw their pathos from the normalcy of physical presence. Our first communication is tactual as befits our being body-words. Tactual presence with others founds our lives and is the hidden support for such an unlikely activity as a philosopher arguing with someone *else* about the possibility of there being other people.

We grow in self-awareness by contrasts that develop between other people and ourselves, but the presence of other people is first. An infant's relations with others enables him, after some time, to become aware of himself as a self. Psychological evidence is unified in contradicting the view that we first know ourselves as persons and on the basis of that knowledge go on to infer the existence of other persons. "Objectivity," we observed, itself implies communication and community.

We are with others for better or for worse. But to be

with others makes demands upon us; the presence of others forces us to make decisions, and those decisions must frequently be as specific as the people who demand them. That is what annoys us. Other people help locate us in the world instead of allowing us to be where we want to be. A responsible father cannot use all of his spare time the way he did before he had a family. In many instances, however, we try to minimize others instead of recognizing them; we feel we can be more ourselves only if we are less involved with them. We think we maximize ourselves by minimizing others. Actually, it is just the opposite, as the previous analysis of love indicates.

To be a human self is to be someone definite with a specific location. To be a person is to express oneself in decisions. By withdrawing from others I therefore deny my true self, for I try to avoid the demand for decision the presence of others forces upon me. There are ambiguities in human life, and frequently there are conflicts among our most cherished principles; there are "hard cases" in ethics where no easy solution presents itself. Frequently, such problems can be avoided if we withdraw as completely as possible from others and try to live our lives in a restricted area. If we confine ourselves completely enough, we may be able to see all of our decisions clearly and so perform them easily. But ease of living purchased at the price of withdrawal from interpersonal relationships is actually a betrayal of our human nature. It stunts personal development in the same way as trying to live in the past does.

So far in this chapter we have used the words "society" and "community" interchangeably; there is much to be said for making a distinction between them, however, and a good number of contemporary thinkers do so. Where the distinction is made, "society" refers to an association of people pursuing their private interests, who are nevertheless bound together by some specialized goal they intend. A society of butterfly collectors will serve as an illustration. Such a group of people has a common bond to the extent that they all collect butterflies; their common function is the basis of their togetherness. But such togetherness is limited by design, and if there is no information or object they are interested in exchanging with one another, there is no basis for their organization. Such people are associates within their society; they need nothing but collecting in common in order for their organization to function smoothly. In a society—and the society need not be limited to such a small group as butterfly collectors; it can as well be an industrial concern, a union, or a nation—one person is replaceable by another, for the immediate concern is for a person's function rather than for himself.

In a community, on the other hand, persons are concerned with each other as persons rather than as functions. Communion rather than utility is the basis of the group, and the people within it view each other as friends rather than merely as associates. The bond of a community is love, and, as Immanuel Kant would have put it, all the people within it are treated as ends in themselves rather than as means to something beyond themselves.

Professor John Macmurray distinguishes society from community in the manner we have just described them. In the light of that distinction, he sees religion itself develop out of the essential interrelationship of persons in community.

In a society where persons are only functionally related to each other, their common purpose (such as collecting butterflies or their mutual protection in the world at large) is enough to hold them together. They are organizationally bound together by their common goal, and that goal is sufficient to assign each person the specific functions he must perform for the good of the whole.

In a community, however, where persons are loved for themselves as persons, a higher principle of union operates. The statement of a limited common purpose is not inclusive enough to cover the interrelations of persons in their totalities as friends; there can be no formally drawn up constitution for a friendship because friends have too much in common to make formal description either possible or necessary. It is not possible to mention everything in an abstract document, and it is needless where the goodwill of the parties toward each other is assured. Constitutions define minimums, and love always seeks the maximum.

The structure of true community is best seen in a pair of friends, which Professor Macmurray calls the basic unit of personal community.[13] In such community, persons must retain their difference and identity, but each realizes himself only through others, for a lover's primary interest is in his beloved, not in himself. Reciprocity and mutual support exist. Having no fear of the other because the bond with the other is love, each person is encouraged

[13] John Macmurray, *Persons in Relation* (New York: Harper and Row, 1961), p. 158.

freely to be himself, and each is *equally* encouraged to be as much himself as possible. Intimidation and harassment are unknown. Thus, true community is constituted by equality and freedom.

Although Professor Macmurray's analysis has been of community, his illustration has been in terms of one pair of friends. If their concern is only for each other, they will have to defend themselves against the ever-present possibility of intrusion by other people. The negativity of defensiveness will thus pervade their personal relationship, making their positive bond of union submissive to it. The positive exercise of their mutuality will then be subverted. Macmurray concludes that the only way a person can fully achieve self-realization is by being positively motivated toward everyone with whom he is related. The ideal of personal living is "a universal community of persons" where each is totally concerned for all the others: in anything less than such a community, unresolved fear of others will be found and freedom will to some degree be destroyed. The possibility of hostility on the part of others will limit self-giving exposure. Thrown back upon ourselves, our own previous analysis indicates that we cease positively to transcend ourselves, and so become less than ourselves. Our bodies and our words become fortifications instead of gates; we contract instead of expand. "The problem of community is the problem of overcoming fear and subordinating the negative to the positive in the motivation of persons in relation."[14] That, in fact, "is the basic problem of all personal life."[15]

[14] *Ibid.*, p. 161.
[15] *Ibid.*

The overcoming of such fear is the work of religion. How?

Only through the idea of a personal Other who stands in the same mutual relation to every member of the community . . . The universal Other must be represented as a universal Agent, whose action unifies the actions of every member of the community, and whose continuing intention is the unity of all their several intentions . . . so that each member can think his membership of the community through his relation to this person, who represents and embodies the intention which constitutes the general fellowship.[16]

We cannot keep from quoting Professor Macmurray further.

The fear of the Other [in this case, not God] is, at bottom, the fear of life; and this has two aspects, which are ultimately one—it is the fear of other people and the fear of Nature. Death is at once our defeat at the hand of the forces of nature and our final isolation from the community of the living . . . the function of religion is as much to transform the fear of Nature as the fear of one's fellows . . . For this reason religious reflection, when it is full-grown, must represent the original personal author of the community as the author of the world; and the life of community as a fellowship of the world—of man with Nature as well as of man with man. Or rather, it must represent the personal community as maintained through an organic harmony between man and the world. The personal must include and subordinate the nonpersonal for the sake of the realization of the personal."[17]

[16]*Ibid.*, p. 164.
[17] *Ibid.*, p. 165.

The understanding of the correlative relationship of man to the world developed in the present book enables Macmurray's point to be made with fresh emphasis and additional justification. Man is relation-to-the-world and is himself only in community; the Author of man must be, then, at one time Author of both world and community. Man can be his full self only in such an Author's presence.

VII ✤ At Supper?

We have seen contemporary thought newly call our attention to the communal nature of man. The world in which we live is a field of meaning; it is a cultural milieu much more than it is a merely external, natural container. We are formed by community through the language we inherit, through the models of ego development with which we are furnished by those around us, through the legal and institutional location provided for us by the society into which we are born. All the attitudes necessary for personal development—trust, support, initiative, identity, intimacy—involve relations with others; the human need for mutuality and reciprocity is the proclamation of man's social nature.

There can be no doubt of the first Christians' awareness of the interpersonal nature of human existence; it was an essential mark of their continuity with the Jews. The Jews, as all primitive people, had a grasp of the communal nature of being which they lived instead of philosophized about. The Jew felt that he was saved only as a member of God's chosen race, the People of Israel. God promised Abram that he would make him "a great nation" (Genesis

12:2). When Abram was given the name Abraham, God told him that he would make him "the father of a multitude of nations" (Genesis 17:5). Again, when God told Jacob to change his name to Israel, God said that "a nation and a company of nations shall come from you" (Genesis 35:11). God repeated his promise when Israel feared to go to Egypt to see his son Joseph (cf. Genesis 46:3). David summed the matter up in his prayer, recounted in the seventh chapter of the Second Book of Samuel: "And thou didst establish for thyself thy people Israel to be thy people for ever; and thou, O Lord, didst become their God" (V. 24).

For the Israelites, *to be* was to-be-with-others. The *others* were other people—and God. When God sent Moses to Pharaoh, God said, "I will be with you" (Exodus 3:12). For all of God's mystery and difference as the I AM, he was known to be somehow present with his people. In the New Testament, when Joseph was told that the son Mary would bear should be called Emmanuel, "God with us" (Matthew 1:23), prophetic expectation (cf. Isaiah 7:14) and God's previous relationship to Israel were understood to be fulfilled, not denied. The Jews thought themselves to be unique among the peoples of the earth and expected "men from the nations of every tongue [to say] 'Let us go with you, for we have heard that God is with you'" (Zechariah 8:23).

The New Testament Church saw itself as the New Israel, God's people (*laos*) or race (*genos*) newly chosen. That is clearly seen in I Peter 2:9-10: "But you are a chosen race, a royal priesthood, a holy nation, God's own people. . . . Once you were no people but now you are

God's people" (cf. also Titus 2:14 and Revelation 21:3).
By comparing Christ to the second Adam, St. Paul sees
Christ as the father of a race and, indeed, of all men (cf. I
Corinthians 15:45, 47).

The essential interrelationship that exists among Christians is clearly seen in such New Testament injunctions as
"Bear one another's burdens, and so fulfill the law of
Christ" (Galatians 6:2) and "For he who loves his neighbor has fulfilled the law. . . . Love does no wrong to a
neighbor; therefore love is the fulfilling of the law"
(Romans 13:8, 10). St. Paul writes that, having been baptized into one body by one Spirit, "if one member suffers,
all suffer together; if one member is honored, all rejoice
together" (I Corinthians 12:26). The First Epistle of St.
John gives us the ultimate criterion for concern for others:
"By this we know love, that he laid down his life for us;
and we ought to lay down our lives for the brethren"
(3:16). The good of one's neighbor should be the constant concern of Christians, for the good of others was the
constant concern of Christ (cf. Romans 15:2 f.).

Christians can be themselves only as members of the
body—and so of the community—into which they are
born by the Spirit. Their most characteristic work is
called a liturgy, a word which means "social action." It
comes from the Greek word *leitourgia*, which itself comes
from the two words *laos* and *ergon* meaning "people" and
"work" respectively. The primary liturgy of the Christian
community is the Holy Eucharist; it is something people
do together to be more together, but not more together as
an isolated group. Jesus Christ came into the world to
save the world, and Christians are in the world for the

same purpose. In the early days of the Church a liturgy was not only something done by the community as a whole; it also referred to work done by an individual or a group for the community as a whole. That is the point that needs to be stressed for present-day Christians. They cannot regard the Eucharist as their private source of grace, either as individuals or as a group: two people—a group—can be as selfish as one person, we have seen. The good for which Christian social action is intended is the good of all men; it is not too much to say that it is the good of the whole universe. The Christians' liturgy is to continue God's creation of the world through their incorporation into his Body-Word, Jesus Christ. In God's community, his people receive his meaning (the Word) in order to manifest that meaning through their bodily lives wherever they are in the universe. As the effectiveness of their bodies is extended through cybernation, electricity, atomic power, and new feats of engineering, the possibilities of a truly Christian universe are increased rather than diminished.

The title of the last chapter was the statement "Let's get together sometime." The title of this chapter was the question, "At supper?" That is a good question. If the friends we talked about in the last chapter do get together, the chances are very good that they will eat and drink something during their visit. If people come to our house, our first mark of hospitality is to offer them something to eat or drink. But we have just been talking in cosmic terms. We were speaking of the Christian's obligation to serve all men and to incorporate the whole universe into God's world. Is not seeing the paradigm of such activity in a supper stretching a casual inclination of man too far?

Actually not. The things people do casually are often the best insights we have into what they are essentially. The free association of ideas is useful in psychology to learn what a person's *real* problems are; the structure of such association is frequently the key to the structure of a person's life. So in the case before us, the structure of what we spontaneously do can give us a good insight into what we basically are.

The naturalness with which we eat with others is the naturalness of being ourselves. The person who habitually eats alone is generally antisocial in all of his behavior. All men need to eat; that common need makes an invitation to dine appropriate under all circumstances. People eat together whether the occasion be a wedding, a funeral, a business or social meeting, a family holiday.

But a meal or a supper is more than the expression of a common need: it is also a way of showing friendship. It is a mark of unity. Although we all must take on some food, we can eat alone and we can choose with whom we want to eat. A meal is an opportunity for free association. We have a chance to ask whomever we want to dine with us, and the person whom we ask has a chance to accept or to refuse. Such an interplay of invitation and response reveals the substance of our personal being. It is mutuality in action. But the invitation and its acceptance are not the full extent of choice in such an event. Under ordinary circumstances, choice extends to what will be served, how it will be served, how people will be seated, and what the table talk will be about. In a meal we are located by each other and called to responsible action within that location.

Because of the large number of options involved in sharing a meal together, such activity has been the primary way men have expressed their unity with one another throughout the history of mankind. Formal dinners of state attest to the signing of peace treaties among nations, but much less hypocritically a child shares his candy bar with a buddy.

Since man must be himself in everything he does, meals have played a central role in his religious history, too. Among the Jews, unity with God was primarily expressed through a ritual meal with him. Only friends share a meal together; to sit at God's table is to be God's friend. So it is that man's final union with God after death has been pictured as a celestial feast. In the Gospel according to St. Luke, at the conclusion of the Last Supper and after Christ had told his disciples that he was among them as one who serves, he continued by saying that he had appointed a kingdom for them that they "may eat and drink at my table in my kingdom" (22:30). Present participation in the final goal of man through the Eucharist is readily understood in such imagery.

We have seen that a Christian can be himself only with the Christian community, and we have noted the communal nature of Christian action in the world, the liturgy. The verb "to celebrate" is frequently associated with the word "liturgy" and, similarly, has obvious communal implications. Christians do not attend the liturgy or watch the liturgy or hear it; they celebrate it. The Latin root of "celebrate" conveys the idea of "public," of action involv-

ing many people. It also connotes the idea of "solemniza-
tion," the doing of something with the full realization of
what is done. Properly to celebrate, then, involves the
public performance of some act with deliberate intention.
To celebrate is to make manifest; it is an attempt both
to proclaim and to realize the nature of something. We
celebrate with a meal, and a meal is a celebration. We
manifest social unity with a meal, and, because of the
interpersonal structure of a meal, it, in turn, intensifies the
unity which occasioned it.

The Holy Eucharist celebrates the social nature of man.
Using the word "dialogue" in a wide sense to indicate any
kind of communication between man and another (be the
other another human being or "nature" to the extent that
the latter affirms or denies our understanding of it by its
response to our experiments), we may say that *the Eucharist is the supreme consecration of the fact that all meaning proceeds from dialogue, that all meaning is communal.* In the Eucharist, the "other" in our dialogue is
God himself, the Source of persons and things. That God's
grace perfects man through social activity agrees not only
with the nature of man as we have previously described it,
but also with the nature of God as determined by Christian revelation. A trinitarian God is himself dialogue and
indicates his nature in his created work.

The sacrificial nature of a meal is another significant
insight which has recently become available to us. Due to
the influence of the Middle Ages, sacrifice was too frequently identified with the death of a victim. Union with
God, not death or destruction in itself, is the true goal of
sacrifice. St. Augustine's definition of it as any work done

so that a person may be united with God is coming back into its own.[1] Louis Bouyer has pointed out that in the earliest times sacrifice did not mean "to make sacred" but "to do what is sacred."[2] In the "doing what is sacred," no act of man had wider acceptance than his participation in a sacred meal. Bouyer claims that the early Christians saw the Eucharist as a sacrifice just

because it was the sacred meal of the Christian community. The texts of the Fathers are so clear and consistent on this point that it can only be denied by a kind of wilful blindness.[3]

The primitive view of sacrifice . . . is the meeting *par excellence* of God and man. It is an act that is inseparably social and individual. Each man feels that he is personally engaged in what is basically a common celebration . . . a common meal makes men appreciate their relation with the cosmos which provides the natural resources for their life. Eating in common is the human act *par excellence,* where society is built up as from within, while each man perfects himself by integrating himself with the universe.[4]

That view of sacrifice is brought to fullness in the Christian Eucharist. The Eucharist is the meeting par excellence between God and man, and it is "inseparably social and individual." Its communal nature is stressed by

[1] Cf. *The City of God,* X:6.
[2] Louis Bouyer, *Rite and Man: Natural Sacredness and Christian Liturgy,* trans. by M. Joseph Costelloe (Notre Dame: University of Notre Dame Press, 1963), p. 79 f.
[3] *Ibid.,* p. 83.
[4] *Ibid.,* p. 90.

the fact that it is the expression of the New Israel, and the cosmic dimension is supplied by the presence in it of the Word by whom all things were made. It is the source from which God's work spreads to the farthest corner of the universe, and it is the means by which the Body is built up from within. Selfishness and narrow defensiveness are foreign to eucharistic living, because in such sacrifice the Church is itself offered in the offering it makes to God.[5]

Through the oneness of the body of which they are all members, Christians are meant to become, through community, nothing less than a single cosmic priest offering the universe to the Father. Christian priesthood is that of a community. Jesus Christ is the one and only High Priest, but all those who are members of his body share his priesthood.

We saw in the last chapter that exclusion is foreign to love. We also saw that love makes others be themselves. The aim of love, then, is to form an all-inclusive community within which each person is provided with the support necessary to be himself. Erich Fromm described love as "productiveness"—when that word was taken in a very broad sense. As Christians, we should not conceive of such productiveness in functional terms alone, for that would make of the Church a society where people are important only because of the jobs they perform. (There are theologians who make that mistake.) The Church is gathered and defined by God's love; the source of its productiveness is God, not us. That is why the Church is a community rather than a society. In it persons are loved for what they are because of what *God* does.

[5] Cf. St. Augustine, *The City of God*, X:6.

To be sure, the Church has something to do; to describe the nature of its task is the purpose of this book. But what the Church must do is possible only because it has already been done. The Christian community is based first of all on God's gift of himself to it; only after that gift, and within its presence, can the Church see its goal. In the community of the New Israel, love (God's choice of us) precedes the functions we can perform for him and for each other. Love must express itself, and expression, we have previously said, is the vocation of man. There is no doubt that we must work for God in the world, but that work is the expression of God's love for us instead of the value we have in our isolated selves for God.

On several occasions we noticed how psychological therapy was predicated upon the interpersonal nature of man. The "talking cure" of psychoanalysis is a means by which a new interpersonal history is produced, and Reality Therapy recognizes the interpersonal foundation of man in its emphasis on the primacy of behavior over attitude. Responsibility is the core of personal relationships, and the location we receive in our lives from other people is a location for responsibility.

Responsibility for others was one of the first marks of the Christian community in New Testament times. Responsibility to others was also a mark of the Church in its early centuries. Sin was seen as an offense against the community; it was the means by which a person separated himself from the Christian family. The result of grave sin was excommunication, exclusion from the sacraments of the Church, especially Holy Communion. Because such exclusion was public, penance was public too. Penance was, in fact, celebrated!

Sin separated a person from the eucharistic activity of the Christian community. After such a person had repented of his sins, done his penance, and received absolution, he was received back into the community where the community was most itself—during the Eucharist. In the East, up to the time of their readmission into the community, penitents were dismissed from the Holy Eucharist immediately after the reading of the lessons; they were only allowed to hear the Word of God calling them to repentance. In the West, such penitents could stay in the back of the church during the whole Eucharist, but they could not receive Communion. The rite of reconciliation occurred immediately after the Gospel, usually on Maundy Thursday—the day on which the institution of the Holy Eucharist is commemorated—so that they could then take part in the complete community action.

Realizing the necessary correlation between loving one's neighbor and taking part in the Holy Communion, based on the admonition of our Lord that if one is offering his gift at the altar and there remembers that his brother has something against him, he should leave his gift before the altar and first go and be reconciled with his brother (cf. Matthew 5:23 f.),

the Fathers of the Church based the commandment to love our neighbors principally on the Eucharist. St. Augustine is a classical example of this, when he writes in his exposition of the eucharistic sermon of Jesus the well-known words: "The faithful acknowledge the body of Christ when they are not ashamed to be the body of Christ themselves. . . . That is why the apostles explain the meaning of this bread to us with the words: 'We who are many are *one* bread, *one* body' (I Cor. 10:17). O sacrament of love! O sign of unity! O bond of love!

Whoever seeks life can find a source of life here. Let him come forward and let himself be incorporated, and he will be given life. Let him not shrink back from the binding of the members to one another. Let him be an honourable member with his own place in the whole. Let him hold on firmly to the body" (Com. on John 26:13; PL 35, col. 1612).[6]

The responsibility of God's people toward and for each other, as well as their extended responsibility for the whole cosmos, is celebrated in the Eucharist. Our consolation by Christ, epitomized in the Eucharist when we eat as friends at his table, is nothing if it is not the expression of our whole lives everywhere. A careful consideration of the first six chapters of the Second Epistle to the Corinthians should convince us that we know Christ only for the sake of others. That statement is not too strong in the light of our analysis of the human condition. Because of the social nature of our being, it can truly be said that we do not "have" Jesus until we are consoling others. To "have" him is to be overflowed by him. The overflowing does not come after the having; it does not take time for God to fill up the emptiness of our lives the way it takes time for a stream to fill up the area behind a dam so that the water can overflow it. The first presence of Christ in us is his overflowing of us; and being the creatures we are, the actual overflowing is a better sign of his presence in us than is our feeling of being filled by him. Too many people have felt filled by God when they have actually been protecting themselves; we call them fanatics. If we discover

[6] Bernard Häring, *A Sacramental Spirituality*, trans. by R. A. Wilson (New York: Sheed and Ward, 1965), p. 152.

Christ in ourselves through the Christian consolation we are able to bring to others, then the dynamic of our lives will involve concrete persons answering concrete persons. We will not be trying to get concrete comfort out of an abstract God. If Christians celebrate in the Eucharist the sameness of their mutual relation to God through Jesus, they will be freed so completely from their fear of each other that they will be able to spend their lives helping others be themselves.

St. Cyprian called the Church the "sacrament of unity." But, from the first centuries of the Church, the Holy Eucharist also was known as the sacrament of unity. St. Paul wrote, "Because there is one loaf, we who are many are one body, for we all partake of the same loaf" (I Corinthians 10:17). The Didache, written no later than the second century, beautifully expresses the relation of the Eucharist to the unity of the Church in the following prayer: "Just as this loaf previously was scattered on the mountains, and when it was gathered together it became a unity, so may your Church be gathered together from the ends of the earth into your kingdom" (9:4).[7] Communion implies community; to have Holy Communion is to have holy community. Thus, the Church through the Eucharist fulfills Israel's vocation, for the Lord proclaimed through Moses: "Say to all the congregation of the people of Israel, You shall be holy; for I the Lord your God am holy" (Leviticus 19:2).

Every celebration of the Lord's Supper is an assembly

[7] *The Apostolic Fathers: A New Translation and Commentary*, Vol. 3: *Barnabas and the Didache*, by Robert A. Kraft (New York: Thomas Nelson and Sons, 1965), p. 166.

of the People of God. No matter how many people actually attend, all of God's people are called by the incarnate Word to hear and express God in the world. No Christian can have a religious life apart from Jesus Christ, and no Eucharist can be celebrated without a dialogue between at least two persons. The very structure of the Eucharist makes it impossible for one person to celebrate it by himself. Christ's statement "Do this in remembrance of me" was made to a group and formed a group. All the sacraments are sacraments of Christian faith and so of the community of faith. It is the community of faith in its liturgical gathering that most clearly shows the nature of the Church. In that gathering the Christian community is made by the Eucharist, but the community also makes the Eucharist its expression. The presence of Christ in the Eucharist makes the Church actual in an event; it enables the unity of God's people to be a matter of experience. By that fact the Eucharist calls the Church to be more than it has been in the world up to that moment.

Through the presence of Christ it conveys, the Holy Eucharist is the Church's constant summons to renewal. That men do so little to renew the Church while they go to the Eucharist (and have done so little for centuries) shows how few Christians of today (and through the centuries) would have recognized Christ if they had lived in his day. Man's failure has always been due to presumptions of godliness. The failure of the Church in its eucharistic vocation is a better proof of the degree of presumption on the part of those who call themselves Christians than it is a disproof of the Eucharist as the focus of Christian living. If the Christ who allowed himself to be crucified is the Christ whose presence is real in the Eucharist, is it so surprising that he does not force salvation upon those who receive him sacramentally anymore than he forced salvation upon those who crucified him on Calvary?

In the Holy Communion, Christians receive the Word who creates, whose purpose in the Holy Communion is to build them up (to nourish them) to create. The food they eat actually creates them. It is a never-ending creation because it involves the infinitude natural to all persons. Moreover, Jesus said "*I* am the bread of life" (John 6:35). In the Holy Communion we do not feed upon exhaustible provisions.

The way to be with someone is to do something with him. We are with Christ by *doing* the Eucharist. That activity is personal in its beginning, middle, and end. In its beginning, we are chosen to come to it, commissioned to perform it, and gathered by the Word of God. In its progression, we are united to the will of the Father as that will was revealed to us in the Son. The Father's will supplies our food and is our food; it is the food of which Christ told his disciples they did not know: "My food is to do the will of him who sent me, and to accomplish his work" (John 4:34). In its end or result, the Eucharist actualizes the Church as the body of Christ, an actualization which will not be complete until the Cosmic Christ perfects his cosmic kingdom.

By means of the Eucharist, the Christian community is always "on the way": it is constantly dynamic and meant to be constantly progressive. The Word as flesh, we said in an earlier chapter, is temporal, still working itself out in time, unfolding historically. The Christian community must always do more thoroughly what the Eucharist enables it to do. It must constantly be in process of becoming more itself. Christian existence is always a "straining forward to what lies ahead" (Philippians 3:13).

St. Gregory of Nyssa in the fourth century said that "it is impossible for our human nature ever to stop moving; it has been made by its Creator ever to keep changing."[8] The Eucharist both supplies us with strength for continual change and is the most intimate presence to us of the Source and Goal of all change. A healthy man can forget the injury of the past in his anticipation of a future goal. St. Paul showed his psychological health when he said that he pressed on "forgetting what lies behind and straining forward to what lies ahead" (Philippians 3:13). Not to do so is necrophilia, a form of the love of death.

Freud talked of a "repetition compulsion," the mechanical repetition of actions in the midst of life. There are people who must have a drink every evening at six; there are people who cannot vary a single item in their routine if they are to avoid obvious anxiety. There are also people who have a repetition compulsion about the Eucharist; they do the same thing in the same way for their same purposes all their lives long. No one can deny that perversion is possible in Christianity; it is all around us. But we can deny that such perversion is *Christian.* The whole structure of the Eucharist as body, word, and community makes that denial for us.

[8] Gregory of Nyssa, *From Glory to Glory: Texts from Gregory of Nyssa's Mystical Writings,* Selected and with an Introduction by Jean Daniélou; trans. and ed. by Herbert Musurillo (New York: Charles Scribner's Sons, 1961), p. 103.

Both the goal and gift of the Eucharist are the unity of the People of God. In the Holy Communion persons are located in a responsible way toward each other by their common location toward God through Christ. By accepting the invitation of the Word to come to God's table, we accept location by another as the nature of our being. If its structure is understood, a person cannot go to the Eucharist to escape the world's problems; he can go there, however, to escape the world's answers.

VIII ✤ Focus for the Future

The words "radical" and "secular" have had it.

Their novelty has worn off; their use has been too frequent; the once-new has become the repetitious. An overstuffed stomach creates no demand for "just one more bite."

Still, it would be a shame if the lasting significance of those words were lost for us because they were overused —sometimes even misused—for a time, just as it would be a shame if men destroyed all of their food supply because they happened to have full stomachs at the moment.

The questions "Who are the true Christian radicals?" and "What does it take to become one?" are still worth asking. Happily, many people who are too concerned about the relation of Christianity and the world to be let down by the passing of a fad continue to ask themselves those questions. Such a desire to be radically, i.e., deeply, Christian is the first culturally discernible sign of life in Christianity for a good many years; some would stretch those years to centuries.

A radical, by definition, must be well-grounded. Where? Where his roots are, of course, for "radical" comes

174

from the Latin word meaning "root." There is no doubt
where we men are rooted: in the world. Whatever is radically new in our lives comes from our new knowledge of
the world and our new relations to the world. Secular
man, at least in one sense, is not a recent invention; if
"secular" is taken in its meaning of "worldly," secular man
is merely man as he lives in the world. Not to be secular in
that sense is not to be man at all. At the deepest level, all
battles among men are battles among secularists.

A person who wants to act as radically as possible must
express himself through his body. Suicide is the supreme
example. Even our lesser radicals feel the obligation to
grow beards and not to visit their barbers; their "social
suicide" shows they are living a life different from that of
"polite society." Acting through the body is the way to
take a stand, to do something definite, for our bodily location is always definite. Our bodies can only be one place
at one time; we are basically committed to be where our
bodies are, simply by being alive.

Completely to hand the keeping of one's body over to
someone else is to make a radical commitment to that
person. God made a radical commitment to men when he
handed over the body of Jesus Christ to them. We must
not think of that commitment as an isolated event which
happened only once, a long time ago, for the body of
Christ is still found on earth in the Church and still being
committed to men in the Holy Eucharist.

The Lord's Supper is the most universal service in
Christendom. Almost every Christian church has some
form of it; but, because of the way it is often referred to as
the *Lord's* Supper, it is prevented from truly belonging to

the people for whom it is intended. It either seems to be
so completely the Lord's that it is not ours, or it appears to
be nothing more than a quaint custom, a several-thousand-
year-old ritual meal, which Christians perpetuate because
it makes them feel less frightened in the world. During the
actual service people usually dress, talk, and act differently; the whole business has no direct relation to the
world in which we live.

If, as has been said, the Holy Eucharist is the central
act of the Christian community, and if, as the Second
Vatican Council noted, the Church itself can be called a
eucharistic fellowship, Christianity must share the nature
of its eucharistic activity. If that activity is quaint, so is
Christianity; and that, in fact, is just the way Christianity
does look to many people. The only consolation in the
world's eyes may be that the strange ritualistic expression
of the Christian cult is most frequently confined to the
group's lodges, called "churches," and does not interfere
in any noticeable way with the world's ongoing activity.
It keeps Christians "off the streets," as we say of any problem group that is out of sight, or it puts them on the
streets when no one else is using them anyway. Even some
members of the Church think that the Holy Eucharist
keeps Christians off the streets and out of the world.

Daniel Callahan, Executive Editor of *Commonweal*,
has recently charged that liturgical reform has not borne
out the claim of the Second Vatican Council that the Eucharist sets the hearts of the faithful afire with the com-
pelling love of Christ.[1] People have not been moved out

[1] Daniel Callahan, "Putting the Liturgy in Its Place," *The National
Catholic Reporter*, August 9, 1967.

of their church buildings into the world. Liturgical scholars know where the difficulty lies, and they are spending a
great deal of effort to show that an understanding of
Christ's eucharistic presence deepens one's understanding
of God's presence in the world. But the problem has not
been solved; people do not seem to understand better how
the action of the liturgy leads to action in the world. At
best, they are being brought to understand the compati-
bility of the two actions. But this is quite a different thing.

Mr. Callahan thinks that

as long as the Church continues to proclaim that the most
efficacious meeting with Christ takes place in the liturgy, then
for just that long will people continue failing to take seriously
the Church's faith that Christ is present in the world. . . . The
solution to this problem does not lie in further refinements of
the liturgy (though they are still desirable). The answer lies in
a sharp devaluation of the liturgy itself, in a refutation of the
council's words that the liturgy is the "source and center of
the Christian life," in a cessation of the vain attempt to make
the Christian community understand the intricate mental
gymnastics necessary to personally experience the purported
link between liturgy and world. I doubt they will ever understand and doubt they will ever take the world as seriously as
the liturgy.[2]

Those are sharp charges, but directly to the point if one
honestly observes the Christian community as a whole
today. Mr. Callahan is a Roman Catholic writing for
Roman Catholics, but his words have significance for all
Christians. What can we say to him?

[2]*Ibid.*

First of all, it may be pointed out that with few exceptions previous discussions of the relation of the liturgy to the world have been led by people whose primary interests were historical. They knew a lot about the development of Christian forms of worship; they knew that contemporary forms of worship were sometimes perverse and often unintelligible to present-day Christians; they knew the need for reform and they sparked that reform. But because of the perspectival nature of human life which we have so frequently described, they were not able to see and do everything at once. They were largely unaware of the secular insights we have discussed which deepen our understanding of the liturgy from another point of view. The impossibility of one person—or one group of persons —doing everything for the Church illustrates the necessity for communal action even in our understanding of communal action.

Secondly, we may point out what "center" and "source" mean when the liturgy is called "the center and source of the Christian life." Christians acknowledge that God is Alpha and Omega, the beginning and the end. There is no absolute source or center anywhere outside of God himself. Christians do not believe that time is cyclic in nature, turning upon itself; but the structure of the life they are called upon to live in time does have circular features— that is, everything in it is connected with everything else. The sacraments, for example, are not isolated activities which are completely themselves by themselves; they flow into and out of each other. The world and the sacraments, as we have tried to indicate in some detail in this book, also flow into and out of each other. New life is first given

to a person in baptism, but *that* life is most itself in eucharistic expression. Through incorporation into Christ's mystical body by baptism, a person first joins the community
called together to celebrate the liturgy; by celebrating the
liturgy of Christ's sacramental body, a person offers himself as a co-worker in God's ongoing act of creation and at
the same time participates in Christ's glorified body, the
personified goal of the new creation. But the glorified body
of Christ, in turn, is essentially one with the mystical body
into which the Christian was first admitted at baptism.
The Christian life in this world is lived within the dialec-
tical interrelation of the three modes of Christ's body:
mystical, sacramental, and glorified.

So it is in the Christian's relation to the world. He can
not make the Holy Eucharist the absolute beginning for
everything, because the Holy Eucharist has secular roots.
On the other hand, the world is not the absolute beginning for everything either, because it is made by God and
becomes fully itself only through man's eucharistic activity.

The liturgy is the source of Christian living in the sense
of being its paradigm, not in the sense of being the button
which, if pushed, makes everything else work automati-
cally. The Holy Eucharist is involvement that perfects involvement; if there is no involvement in the first place,
there is nothing for it to perfect. It is not fire sent to
amaze people by burning in a vacuum. We have seen that
we must be our bodies before we can perfect them; in an
analogous sense, we must be doing something in God's
world before the Eucharist can perfect that action. Secular insights can help Christians understand their relation

to the Eucharist by showing them that their bodily presence alone *is* the making of the world. The perfection the
Eucharist offers to the activity we cannot help but perform by virtue of our existence is intimacy with Christ in
carrying it out; such intimacy is personal rebirth and
never-ending motivation for self-giving.

Our analysis has shown that the same activity is going
on within and outside the Eucharist. Man is body, word,
and community wherever he is; differences in those activities arise only from differences in the degree of their consecration, that is, from differences in the degree of explicit
thankfulness to God found in them. In their eucharistic
setting the thankfulness found in them is Jesus Christ
himself. Continuity rather than sameness would perhaps
be a better way of describing the relationship of activities
that take place within and outside the eucharistic framework, for through consecration an activity becomes different from itself. It becomes God's presence; it becomes
God's gift. That is how eucharistic activity can be at the
same time common to all men and also distinctively
Christian. Taken in one way, the People of God includes
all people at all times and at all places; so taken, every
person in the history of the world is related to the Church.
There are degrees of participation in the Church because
there are degrees of men's explicit cooperation with God's
will. If, as we have suggested, the Church is a eucharistic
fellowship, it follows that the same degrees of participation must be admitted in the Eucharist as are admitted in
the Church. That has not yet been done in any telling
way, but if the Holy Eucharist is rooted as basically in the
life of men as we have claimed, the conclusion is both
proper and necessary.

We must think big! We must get the big picture! If we do not, it shows that our "God is too small." In the cosmic, world-forming perspective of the Eucharist, what was once thought to be correct may no longer be so. Is the Last Supper finished? Yes, as the source of denominational rivalry (for the Eucharist is the source of unity); yes, as a Church *possession* (for the Eucharist is the structure of the Church); yes, as an exclusive diner's club (for the Eucharist is a charge to serve others). The work of the Church is in the world, and the work of the Eucharist is there too. If the divine liturgy turns us outward toward God's continuing creation of the cosmos, our eucharistic problems will change.

In the once-held view that the creation of the world is finished and that God has committed himself to the Church for safekeeping, protecting God from other men (especially, as it was patronizingly put, for their own sakes!) had some justification. In a dynamic view of reality in which God is understood still to be creating his world through us, our protection of him in the world loses the propriety it was once thought to have. Believing in the real presence of Christ in the Eucharist, can limitation of his exposure to the problems of men be justified in the administration of the sacrament? Have Christians so treasured Christ in the Eucharist that they have inadvertently isolated him from the conditions of human existence? If so, Christians have disguised Christ's nature in their acknowledgment of his presence. In many instances the defense of Christ's eucharistic presence in metaphysical and abstract terms seems to have replaced the awareness of Christ's presence for what he personally and morally is. Christ's *death* showed the degree of God's availability to the world. Even though the Father let his Son be killed by men, many Christians have become concerned not to let the Son confront honest differences among themselves. Whom are they fooling? We may well wonder if some Christians can be content to let God win his victory his way. It never occurs to them that God's victory, which was won in spite of man, might escape man's showcase. What significance does the Son we kill by our sins see in our fragmented protection of him?

We must still have norms in the world to judge the acceptance of Christ, for the Christian religion means one thing rather than another; it is not a formless blob of equivocal goodwill. The unity to which we are called in Christ involves the whole man, making explicit demands on his reason and power of judgment. But the norms themselves must primarily witness to God's *gift* to us in Christ; they must witness to the *total* dependence we have on him in doing his work. Christ's presence in the world is a call to something definite, and our response to it creates a community of faith. Where such community can be recognized among people who are already members of Christ's body through baptism, why should they not be fed together by Christ's sacramental body for their common work in the world?[3] The will of God for his people

[3] To be sure, some problems remain, for example, those concerning the relationship of the special priesthood of ordained men to the general priesthood of all Christians in the eucharistic celebration and those concerning the different sacramental concepts of the ministry in the churches. Such problems cannot be overlooked, but, in a number of instances, a concelebration of the Eucharist may be possible without compromising the participants' integrity if the Eucharist's cosmic orientation is sufficiently realized; the Eucharist is primarily a means of getting beyond ourselves in God's world, not of proving ourselves to other men.

is the substance of every Christian activity, including the Eucharist. We do not deal with *different things* in Christianity but with one thing—God's will—considered at one time from the point of view of the Church, at another time from the point of view of the Eucharist or the remaining sacraments or the Word or mission to the world. God's will is one through them all.

Whatever we are that is godly should be celebrated. We are what we are in order to celebrate it; where a community of faith exists in God's eyes, it should be able to celebrate itself in the world for what it is. Certainly the Holy Eucharist proclaims a unity that already exists within God's people in addition to effecting a unity which does not yet exist. But if we remember that the unity it perfects is the unity of the Body, I think a good case can be made for saying that it is the baptismal faith—the faith that first admits to the Body—which is the sufficient faith for admission to Holy Communion.[4] There is a "hierarchy

---

The important thing is the manifestation of Christian community *where it exists in God's eyes rather than in our canon law*. Entrance into a solemn covenant to seek further unity may make eucharistic participation possible among churches that are juridically separated at the moment. The one thing that absolutely *cannot* be tolerated is eucharistic participation or concelebration that does not intend the increased unity of the Church. To use the Eucharist to perpetuate the present divisions of Christendom or to minimize the scandal of the status quo would be the gravest perversion.

[4] Detailed problems arise here about the role of confirmation. Traditionally, it was part of the initiatory rite. Its greatest ecumenical problem involves the nature and role of episcopacy in the Church. However, no theological contradiction is involved in receiving Holy Communion, especially under unusual circumstances, before confirmation or without it. We are speaking, at the moment, about the reception of Holy Communion; the celebration of the Eucharist brings up additional problems

of truths," as the Second Vatican Council put it: not everything one man accepts as the truth can be required of another man if discipline is going to be invoked in the name of God. There are legitimate diversities within the Church, for the Church as we know it is in the world, and the human world is, by definition, one of different perspectives. The very protection the Eucharist has often received in the past indicates a gross *underestimation* of its real value. The Eucharist is in one sense too constitutive of our being to be protected by us.

If the nature of the Eucharist, the fact of Christ's presence in it, and the means of effecting that presence can be essentially agreed upon by members of the mystical body, might not their common reception at the Table of the Lord—with the selflessness such participation involves— be the primary means by which God wills to bring about ever-increasing unity among his people? St. Paul said that we are one body *because* we partake of one loaf (I Corinthians 10:17).

Is it possible to eat together at God's table and not grow together in unity? Not if we realize that we are eating at *God's* table and realize the communal destiny we necessarily have as *incarnate* persons. God's task for us is so great and so inclusive—and we already share in it so basically —that a great deal of the former exclusiveness of men among themselves can find no basis. We are not sufficient enough in ourselves, and we do not have such sufficiency

---

pertaining to orders of ministry. Even there new solutions to old problems may eventually be found through increased emphasis on the primacy of the faith community in sacramental matters and an acknowledgment of degrees of participation in the traditional threefold orders of ministry.

in Christ, to choose isolation as a viable option in the world. If we realize the intersubjective nature of our primary location in the world, we will all better understand God's intention for us in the Church. To see that we are already and necessarily engaged in a common work with all men because of our bodies, and that God in Christ came to consecrate *that* work, is the prerequisite necessary for seeing the role of the Eucharist in our lives.

Dr. Glenn T. Seaborg, Chairman of the Atomic Energy Commission in the United States, recently wrote an article entitled "The Cybernetic Age: An Optimist's View."[5] After describing the possible effects of cybernation in such areas of our lives as transportation, medical diagnosis, and the amount of leisure available to us, Dr. Seaborg concluded that a major reevaluation of our goals and values is needed. He hoped that the results of such analysis "may provide us with something like a comprehensive philosophy of life to match the physical unity of mankind rapidly being fostered by today's science and technology."[6] In the cybernetic age ever-increasing responsibility will fall upon our university communities. They will be sources of social change, but they themselves will also have to change. While continuing work in specialized areas, they will also have to foster interdisciplinary thinking. Man's need for wisdom increases with his rapidly expanding knowledge; education in the coming cybernetic revolution must be toward "total living" rather than merely "earning a living."

There are people who believe that human incentives

[5] *Saturday Review*, July 15, 1967.
[6] *Ibid.*, p. 23.

will diminish in a "cybernated utopia," but Dr. Seaborg is not among them. He feels that machines will ultimately help men in their interpersonal relations.

. . . when machines have truly freed us from the necessity of physical work, perhaps we can better accept them for what they are and have the time to see and relate to other people in a different light. When we have more time to be with other people—not accidentally, on crowded buses, in elevators, in markets and offices, but in places of our own choosing at our own leisure—we may feel differently toward one another.

When we are less likely to be in competition with one another, much of the hypocrisy of society will vanish and more honest relationships will be formed. And, finally, when we can walk down the street—anywhere in the world—in a community free from want, where every human being has a sense of dignity not gained at the expense of others, we might not only walk free from fear but with a great feeling of exaltation.

If we can make the transition of living with and using the complex machines of the future in a *human-oriented* society, the rewards will be worth any effort we can make. As everyone knows, such a transition will not be easy, because it involves so much of what Eric Hoffer has called "The Ordeal of Change." But I think we will have to make such a transition eventually. We may have already begun to do so.[7]

A grand picture; we may hope it comes true. But the description Dr. Seaborg gives us is filled with "may's" and "if's." Philosophy, science, and education are the activities

[7] *Ibid.*

Dr. Seaborg bases his optimism upon; not once does he mention the role of religion in the future. Can philosophy, science, and education do the job? If we extrapolate from their record to date, we will project pessimism, not optimism. Some of the effects of Dr. Seaborg's "cybernetic utopia" are already experienced in many suburban streets: young people with almost total leisure (at least in summer) live "in a community free from want." But human problems in the suburbs seem to be increasing rather than decreasing. By the very fact that they have so much and are so "free," many suburban parents cannot believe that *their* children are in trouble even after they are in trouble. Behavior patterns do not necessarily improve in want-free streets on the basis of the empirical evidence at our disposal.

Even a cybernetic age needs God, and God, it seems to me, has already given the cybernetic age what it needs—the pattern for truly personal living. Cybernetics may aid our return to a more personally concerned society, because it requires that we think in sets, types, and wholes rather than in a linear, mechanical way. But the ultimate question is this: What types will such an age adopt? I suggest that eucharistic living gives us the type of patterned living our own cybernated inventions are pointing the need for. We have seen that we *are* a pattern of organizing space and time; that pattern takes shape through our bodies, words, and communities. The "physical unity of mankind" Dr. Seaborg mentions is both drawn upon and perfected in our understanding of the eucharistic Body; the linguistic communication which founds education finds its source and goal in the eucharistic Word; the fear of one another which Dr. Seaborg only hopes will be removed is made actually impossible in the eucharistic community.

The Holy Eucharist gives the ultimate reason for what Dr. Seaborg wants to happen actually to happen. The Eucharist brings something to the cybernetic age which that age cannot supply for itself: it brings the motivation, strength, and reason necessary to turn cybernetically produced possibilities into godly actualities.

Human life requires mutuality, full personal presence physically expressed. Such mutuality cannot be produced by machines, even cybernated ones, and the community of men cannot experience such mutuality as a community apart from relations to a transcending Person. Our total needs can never be met by anything in this world.

Each of us knows that only he is himself; as a self he is irreducible. That fact alone shows that the gift of himself to someone else is irreducible to an abstract, and therefore general, theory about his presence. Even if his presence is predicted, the way he is actually present has a dimension totally escaping the prediction. To hold someone's hand is different from the prediction that you will hold his hand. Ask any girl who wants to be married but is not. The gift involved in personal presence is the liberating dimension of Christianity. Only when that dimension is recognized can a person begin to be a Christian, for the common testimony of all Christians, emphasized so strongly by St. Paul, is that in choosing God I realize for the first time that he has already chosen me.

Gift! Chosen! Those acts constitute the Christian's world. The gift of Jesus Christ to us is God's choice of us.

To be so chosen is to be located in God's will: life in Jesus Christ gives us the type of special location we need in order to be persons. But in this instance our location frees us in the world instead of confining us. Since our being as a whole is chosen by God through the incarnation of his Son, we know that we are chosen wherever our being is. We have a secure location in personal concern which enables us to be God's agents no matter what our worldly location may happen to be.

There is a basic sense in which Christianity is summarized in the concept of "being chosen." Nowhere can that summary be more clearly seen than in the Eucharist, about which Christ himself said, "Do this . . ." Choice is an activity which activates; being chosen makes a difference in the life of the person chosen. If a boy chooses a girl to dance with him, all she can do is dance. The secret doubts she had before the dance are immediately overcome by that single act.

We all long to be chosen, and most of us know the thrill which accompanies such choice. Even such an apparently small thing as being among the first players picked for a softball team in grade school can have lasting effects. The boys so chosen are carried beyond themselves; they are anxious to throw themselves into the game. Even to be chosen next to the last is important to us, because such a person is still chosen. The last boy remaining goes to a team by default; but once on a team, he tries to identify with the chosen by his kidding and nonchalance so that he can at least achieve a vicarious identity in the group. We all need acceptance, and acceptance is a form of choice.

By choosing us, God makes himself the answer to our problems, freeing us from ourselves. We then embody freedom instead of searching for it. In Christ, history saves us from history: God's personal act saves us from our personal limitations. His decision swallows our indecision. To be chosen by God is to live in his world beyond ourselves; it is to be buoyed up by his constant newness.

Moreover, in Christ Jesus we are not chosen once by God and then left alone the way a small boy may be left out of tomorrow's baseball team. Jesus Christ's continuing life with the Father is the Father's continuing choice of us; that is the significance of Easter. Choice, considered just in itself, is an activity; past choice is no longer choice. Choice is love, and God is love. The stability our lives find in God's choice of us is grounded in his eternal nature as perfect love.

The kerygmatic nature of Christianity is emphasized in the description of that religion we have just given. Christianity must be proclaimed as Good News because something has happened in the world which is newsworthy. God has acted in the world with the reality of the world; by so doing he has newly made the world his own in a way that makes the world new. But glimpsing the new world which is centered in Christ's body, our responsibility for the ungodly condition of the old world is highlighted: it is the recognition of such responsibility that makes the first Christian act one of repentance.

The kerygma (proclamation) of the earliest Church was a call to men to repent, assurance of the forgiveness of sins because of Christ's resurrection from the dead, and a new life actualized by the gift of the Spirit. Christians today must understand that in those simple, personal terms—responsibility recognized in repentance, loving forgiveness in Christ, life in the Spirit—the universe is to become God's world. To live in God's world is the most intimate relation we can have with him, because it involves the most constant, most ubiquitous, and most fundamental feature of our being: our lived insertion into reality. The kerygma calls us to a direct, personal relationship with God, and in that relationship nothing less than the creation of the cosmos continues.

Our task is twofold: we must not let cosmic descriptions of Christianity keep us from the personal (and, in that sense, simple) wellspring of our power; on the other hand, we must never think that our personal relationship with God is so simple that it can be isolated from its cosmic goal. If we understand the true nature of eucharistic living, these two poles will be kept in proper balance.

By freely instituting the sacrament of the Holy Eucharist, Christ was, in effect, choosing us in a unique and worldly way. That choice was an act of love which gave something radically new to us; it was a choice meant to move us beyond ourselves. Still, it was also a choice of us, a choice whose call fits the most characteristic features of our being. No greater gift could be given us than that of letting us help create God's world by being what we are: body, word, and community.